Chatham Village

Chatham Village

Panoramic view of the early Chatham Village

ANGELIQUE BAMBERG

Pittsburgh's Garden City

UNIVERSITY OF PITTSBURGH PRESS

Published by the University of Pittsburgh Press, Pittsburgh, Pa., 15260
Copyright © 2011, University of Pittsburgh Press
All rights reserved
Manufactured in the United States of America
Printed on acid-free paper
10 9 8 7 6 5 4 3 2 1

Text design and typesetting by Kachergis Book Design

Library of Congress Cataloging-in-Publication Data
Bamberg, Angelique.
Chatham Village : Pittsburgh's Garden City / Angelique Bamberg.
    pages cm
Includes bibliographical references and index.
ISBN 978-0-8229-4406-5 (cloth : alk. paper)
1. Chatham Village (Pittsburgh, Pa.) 2. Planned communities—
Pennsylvania—Pittsburgh. 3. Architecture and society—
Pennsylvania—Pittsburgh—History—20th century. 4. Stein,
Clarence S. 5. Wright, Henry, d. 1936. 6. Chatham Village
(Pittsburgh, Pa.)—Buildings, structures, etc. 7. Pittsburgh (Pa.)—
Buildings, structures, etc. I. Title.
HT169.57.U62C493 2011
307.76'809748'86—dc22
        2010045466

Contents

Preface

Tucked onto a wooded hillside in Pittsburgh, Pennsylvania, a quiet neighborhood of brick row houses and park-like open space testifies to the enduring importance of a housing revolution that wasn't. Chatham Village was built in response to a litany of socioeconomic conditions that sounds eerily familiar: scarcity of jobs and resources, disorienting technological change, distrust of government control, and anxiety about the dangers and discontents of cities twinned with attraction to their unique advantages of density, culture, and community. It grew out of the vision of two of the most brilliant urban planners of their generation, Clarence Stein and Henry Wright, and a social crusader, Charles Lewis, who sat at the helm of Pittsburgh's newly formed Buhl Foundation.

As the Great Depression settled on the United States, Lewis had set out to demonstrate a solution to his city's acute shortage of decent, affordable housing. Like Stein and Wright, he was ahead of his time in his concern about the wasteful environmental effects of sprawling subdivision construction; unlike them, however, he rejected the role of government and philanthropy in assuming responsibility for sheltering the lower classes. Lewis believed that private enterprise was the economic expression of democracy and had the ability to solve any problem, if given incentives and shown the way.

Through Chatham Village, Lewis wanted to model how private builders could build high-quality new housing for people of modest means who usually lived in tenements or in places "handed down" from the upper classes once they had lost their luster. These working-class residents, Lewis held, constituted a unique market in which private developers could make a profit.

To help him demonstrate this, Lewis hired Clarence Stein and Henry Wright, both architects and housing reform advocates who designed entire communities inspired by the belief that the built environment could transform the way people lived. Stein and Wright did not believe that only the wealthy should be able to afford beauty and quality. At the same time, they were cognizant of the importance of housing that was affordable to build as well as to occupy, and their plans for well-designed communities always strove to reduce construction costs without sacrificing residential amenities.

Stein and Wright were influenced by the utopian ideals of Ebenezer Howard, a Londoner whose book, *Garden Cities of To-morrow,* promoted the planning and construction of low-density, large-scale zoned communities, organized around a central park, in which people would be able to enjoy the best of both town and country. Beginning in the 1920s, Stein and Wright engaged deeply with Howard's theories, applying and adapting them to their own evolving vision of a modern American town. Howard considered the preservation of nature paramount, streets the most wasteful form of open space, and speculative real estate development deadly to a humane living environment. Accordingly, Stein and Wright's typical housing plan sought to replace the urban grid with organic layouts of streets and houses which responded to the natural features and contours of their sites. The dwellings they specified were small, often connected, clustered around swaths of communal lawns and gardens, and linked by pedestrian pathways. Perimeter roadways delivered vehicles to the edges of a community but did not crosscut its park-like inte-

rior. Even as they strove to design a retreat from the modern
metropolis, Stein and Wright were preoccupied with accom-
modating automobiles, as well as electricity, telephones, and
other technological innovations that promised to transform
life in the early twentieth century. Their community designs
were among the first to anticipate the ways in which this
would happen.

Lewis wanted Stein and Wright to design the Buhl Foundation's housing project because they believed, as he did, that
physical and social planning could be synthesized in one integrated discipline, and that architectural and planning solutions could help to address complex social problems. These
men put their hearts, their minds, and their money into the
concept that if everyone only had the perfect place to live, the
world would truly be a better place.

It is easy to view this as naïve. Eighty years after Chatham Village was announced as a demonstration in for-profit
planned residential development, it has never been replicated
on the scale its creators envisioned, and its influence has
largely been diluted to a set of à la carte concepts in modern
subdivision design. Pittsburgh and other American cities have
changed in ways that Lewis, Stein, and Wright could not have
imagined, as have larger patterns of urban and suburban
housing. Chatham Village has changed from a rental community run for profit by a private foundation to a cooperative
owned by a nonprofit corporation of its residents, who constitute a different demographic group than the original tenants
of 1932.

Yet the more things have changed at Chatham Village,
the more they have stayed the same. Through the thoroughness of its planning, the genius of its site design, and the deliberate investment in high-quality construction, Chatham
Village has remained a stable, attractive, desirable community
for over the better part of a century. As the fortunes of the
conventionally built city around it have fluctuated, Chatham
Village has held its value.

Shortly after Chatham Village was completed, its planners Clarence Stein and Henry Wright ended their partnership over professional and personal differences. In 1936, Wright died. Forty years later, the *New York Times* eulogized Stein, hailing him as a forgotten prophet. The last of just three projects designed by the partnership of Stein and Wright, Chatham Village is the only one to be fully built according to its original plan and to remain intact despite changes in ownership, occupancy, and societal expectations of housing. As such, it is a testament to the particular genius of Stein and Wright's collaboration and the endurance of their community planning ideals. But it is more than a historical artifact. It is a living community in which the original planning and design have, remarkably, required only the finest of tuning to adapt to the twenty-first century.

The ideas and ideals upon which Chatham Village was built are still relevant today: quality, community, affordability, and conservation, to name a few. At a time when suburban sprawl, smart growth, affordable housing, and sustainable development are part of our national vocabulary of concern, Stein and Wright's final and fullest collaboration reveals how the comprehensive planning of communities can shape the way we live, even if it doesn't revolutionize the way we build.

Acknowledgments

Research and writing can be solitary work, but bringing this book to fruition has been a process of consultation, collaboration, and, at times, reliance on the kindness of strangers. I would like to acknowledge the time and talents of those whose contributions were essential.

I owe a debt of enduring gratitude to Michael Tomlan and Kermit C. Parsons. Michael's encyclopedic knowledge, insightful prodding, and unflagging support helped me frame this story. K. C., too, contributed mightily to the shape and breadth of my work, beginning with his observation that Chatham Village deserved a thorough study of its own, which set me on this path. I dearly wish he were here to read this book, and I dedicate it to his memory.

I am deeply thankful to many people in Chatham Village for, literally, opening doors to me there. David Vater, who knows more about Chatham Village than anyone, gave me personal tours, introductions, and, time and again, the benefit of his profound understanding of his community. I cannot thank him enough. Allen Benton, Dot and Gene Gundrum, Connie Kaiser, Abe Vestal, and Mary Williams welcomed me into their homes and shared generously of their time and recollections. Kathryn Nelson was also very helpful over the phone. I extend my thanks, too, to Sandy Richard at the

Shalercrest Housing Association for generously illuminating many aspects of life in that community.

I am grateful to Edward Muller at the University of Pittsburgh for connecting me with Cynthia Miller at the University of Pittsburgh Press. By doing so, he set this process in motion, and in his review of subsequent drafts, he helped me to tell a more complete, cohesive story. I would also like to thank Cynthia for continuing to believe in this project even as it went adrift from time to time. Her confidence that I had a story to tell was bolstering.

The Buhl Foundation, which built Chatham Village so many years ago, is still doing good work in Pittsburgh. I am personally very grateful for its generous support of the production of this book, which has surely made it better. It is a reflection, as well, on the professional talents of the editors at the press who shepherded my manuscript to publication with insight and commitment. In particular, Peter Kracht supplied a confident vision for the book, Deborah Meade edited it with a judicious eye for structure and detail, and Colleen Heavens was tireless in her efforts to locate, organize, and gain permissions for the illustrations that help to tell the story.

Kirk Savage, Linda Hicks, Natalie Swabb, and the rest of the History of Art and Architecture Department at the University of Pittsburgh ensured that I had access to the university resources I needed to complete this project when I needed them. That has been invaluable to me.

Many archivists and librarians made my research a pleasure, among them Martin Aurand at the Carnegie Mellon University Architecture Archive, the staff of the Historical Society of Western Pennsylvania, Barbara Prior at Cornell, and Ray Anne Lockard in the Frick Fine Arts Library at the University of Pittsburgh.

Thank you to Kristin Larsen, a fellow traveler both literally and figuratively, for accompanying me in the discovery of Shalercrest and for sharing her knowledge of critical aspects of Clarence Stein's career; to Michael Goodhart and Renee

Piechocki for their guidance and encouragement at crucial junctures; and to Katherine Zeltner, who was there at the beginning, for her constant friendship and support.

To say that my husband, Jason Roth, also supported this project is a gross understatement. He believed in this book when I despaired. He participated, enthusiastically, in an itinerary of planned community–touring that would have brought a lesser person to his knees. Visiting those places with him and benefiting from his insights vastly deepened my appreciation for the accomplishments of those communities' planners. Jason also read every draft of my work, and his comments always pointed the way toward a better organized, clearer, and more focused narrative.

Finally, I offer my heartfelt thanks to my parents and my children, whose love and support are my bedrock.

Chatham Village

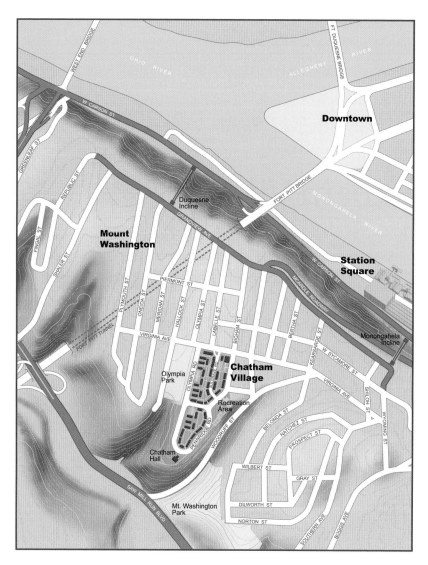

Chatham Village's location in Pittsburgh

one　The Architects of a Solution

In the year of the stock market crash that precipitated the Great Depression, a fledgling foundation in Pittsburgh undertook a bold new mission: to revolutionize American residential development. The Buhl Foundation's emphasis on privately produced, for-profit housing resisted the leftward movement of the 1930s political economy, as increasing rates of unemployment and housing foreclosure ushered in a groundswell of support for government-provided services—including, eventually, public housing. By building a brand-new, privately financed community according to the most progressive planning ideas of the day, the Buhl Foundation sought to provide a model for socially and environmentally responsible capitalism at a time when and in a place where adequate housing was in desperately short supply.

The resulting community, Chatham Village, created a sensation among architects, planners, housing experts, and house-hunters from its initial construction in 1932 until World War II brought new housing production, private and public alike, to almost a complete halt. Chatham Village's 197 red-brick row houses, nestled among private courtyards and park-like woods atop a bluff overlooking Pittsburgh's downtown, were a new kind of response to one of the most dire urban housing crisis situations in the country. Pittsburgh's problems had begun before the Depression swept the rest of the United States. Even during the city's boom years, around the turn of the twentieth century, investors had not put much capital into housing, and since 1910, Pittsburgh's economy had been declining along with its major industries of coal and steel. No new major commerce had moved in to compensate for the loss, and unemployment stood at 5 to 10 percent.[1]

After World War I, a nationwide housing shortage exacerbated the effects of Pittsburgh's industrial and economic decline on the city's residential market. Low vacancy rates, inflation of the costs of construction and building materials, rising rental and purchase prices, and the withdrawal of speculative capital all combined to bring about the collapse of the private building industry across the United States. With no governmental structure to compensate for this failure, there ensued an acute shortage of adequate urban shelter.[2]

Contrary to initial expectations, and despite abnormally low vacancy rates and high demand, the building industry did not recover quickly. Deterred by the scarcity of capital and the inflationary costs of construction, commercial builders did not immediately resume activity on a large scale after armistice. By 1919–1920, however, an industrial and commercial

Figure 1.1. View of downtown Pittsburgh from Mt. Washington, 1932

building boom created a demand for labor, supplies, and capital. Construction costs and rents climbed far above their pre-
war levels, peaking in 1920 and remaining fixed at a perma-
nently high plateau for several years. The nation's residential
building trade, consisting of myriad small, local house builders, was unable to compete for labor and supplies in this market. In 1920, the Pennsylvania Chamber of Commerce Housing Bureau observed that the "shortage of homes has reached
such stupendous proportions that what was formerly a social
question . . . has come to be a real live economic problem—an
industrial menace," since enough workers to drive the economy could not be decently housed. By 1924, according to a
survey of 178 cities conducted by the National Industrial Con-

Figure 1.2. Crowded city neighborhood, probably in New York, used by the editors of *Architectural Forum* in 1932 to dramatize the post–World War I shortage of housing for urban workers.

ference Board, rents were 85 percent higher than they had
been at the start of the war.[3] In June 1931, President Hoover
held a nationwide conference on Home Building and Home
Ownership at which the Committee on Large Scale Operations reported, "The houses of the country constitute our
largest mass of obsolete and discredited equipment."[4]

The post–World War I dwelling shortage was a watershed
in the history of American housing development. Characterized by an acute imbalance of supply and demand, construction costs and affordable rents, the housing emergency of the
1920s discredited the ideas of earlier Progressive reformers,
who had tended to focus upon the sanitary and social pathol-
ogy of the slums and looked to restrictive building and zoning
codes to promote better housing. The postwar crisis launched
a continuing search for alternatives that would provide an
adequate supply of affordable, decent housing for low- and
middle-income Americans. Writer and urban theorist Lewis
Mumford noted that the building industry collapse "gave a
fresh incentive to the housing movement and pushed it along
paths that the older housing reformers never envisaged."[5]

One of these paths, though not an entirely new one, was
the limited-dividend housing corporation, which developed
housing for profit, but limited its return to a relatively low
percentage of its receipts. By dedicating a larger proportion of
its investment to the production of the housing itself, in theory, such a corporation created superior dwellings to those
that a fully commercial developer would build for the same
amount of money.

The limited-dividend mode was called "investment philanthropy" when it was first introduced in England in 1845 by
the frankly named Metropolitan Association for Improving
the Dwellings of the Industrial Classes. Boston citizens
showed interest in limited-dividend development at an 1846
meeting to discuss the establishment of "chartered or private
companies, to procure the construction of large, well-fitted
buildings, especially designed for the use of [the poorer class]

of tenants,"[6] and in 1871, a group of shareholders formed the limited-dividend Boston Cooperative Building Company. In the United States, limited-dividend companies were concentrated in New York City and most often developed multi-family tenement housing, but some also constructed one- and two-family homes in Boston, Cincinnati, Philadelphia, and Washington, D.C. Though a tiny proportion of the housing industry as a whole, limited-dividend companies created residences for thousands of Americans between the mid-nineteenth and the early twentieth centuries.[7]

In 1929, the Buhl Foundation, a one-year-old philanthropy in Pittsburgh, incorporated as a limited-dividend corporation for the purpose of developing Chatham Village. As part of its general mission of civic betterment, the foundation's first director, Charles Fletcher Lewis (1890–1971), convinced its managers to underwrite the construction of a model community for members of Pittsburgh's middle class who had been prevented, first by the housing crisis and then by the Depression, from finding affordable housing outside the city's squalid urban slums.

Lewis was born in Gibsonton, Pennsylvania, and, from an early age, displayed both a strong sense of moral purpose and an interest in newspaper writing. In his early twenties, he abandoned the teaching career for which he had trained to become a professional journalist. Lewis worked as a reporter at the *Oil City Derrick*, a nationally recognized trade paper, and the *Pittsburgh Sun* before moving on to hone his editorial skills at the *Franklin Evening News*. Lewis worked hard and learned quickly, and in 1919, just eight years after his start in journalism, he returned to the *Pittsburgh Sun* as its chief editorial writer.

The only independent newspaper in Pittsburgh, the *Sun* served as a progressive voice for political action in a city stagnating under the leadership of an entrenched Republican machine. Arthur E. Braun, the *Sun*'s owner, believed passionately in Pittsburgh's future as a great modern city and used his

Figure 1.3. Charles Fletcher Lewis

newspaper to promote civic awareness and to champion reform. Charles Lewis fit well into Braun's milieu. An ardent,
idealistic young man, he admired Woodrow Wilson, Jane Ad-
dams, Elihu Root, and Judge Ben Lindsey, the founder of the
juvenile justice system in the United States. Lewis's writing
sought to educate his readers, all of whom he considered potential reformers, about causes including better housing for
low- and middle-income workers and the need for playgrounds and other public recreational space in and near Pittsburgh. He also urged the community to support scholarships
for needy students and the creation of a nonpartisan bureau
of governmental research.[8] In larger arenas, Lewis supported
Democratic candidates for public office and the League of Na-
tions, whose creation he regarded as "the supreme moral issue
of the century."[9]

Lewis's progressive politics and sense of high moral pur-

Figure 1.4.
Henry Buhl Jr.

pose also fit the mission of the Buhl Foundation, founded in
1927 after the death of Henry Buhl Jr. Buhl had become a mul-
timillionaire as a partner in Boggs and Buhl, a Pittsburgh department store that was one of the largest in the country.
Rich and childless, upon his death Buhl left an estimated $11
million bequest to establish and endow a philanthropic foundation, in memory of his wife, Louise, for the betterment of
the city.

The terms of Buhl's bequest were exceptionally open. Before his death, he had personally selected a four-member
board of managers and entrusted them with complete control
over all future decisions regarding the investing and spending
of the foundation's assets. Buhl placed no official restrictions
on the types of causes to benefit from the foundation's giving,
but in a letter of advice to the board, expressed a general de-

sire to further the progress of public health and medical research, promote national patriotism, and help the poor.

The foundation's four original managers were all local leaders familiar with the business and social climate of the community. As it happened, the most powerful of them was Arthur E. Braun. Recognizing the suitability of his chief editorial writer for the position of executive director, Braun engineered Lewis's appointment to that position in 1928, and Lewis remained director of the foundation until his retirement in 1956.

Lewis regarded the provision of decent shelter as a moral imperative of capitalist investors. Shortly after assuming the helm of the Buhl Foundation, he researched developments by the limited-dividend City Housing Corporation in New York and secured the managers' permission to study the prospects for initiating similar projects in Pittsburgh. To guide him in this endeavor, Lewis hired three expert consultants, Clarence Stein, Henry Wright, and Frederick Bigger. All were architects, planners, and housing reform advocates who belonged to an informal think tank known as the Regional Planning Association of America (RPAA), founded by Stein in 1923.

The lifetime of Clarence Stein (1882–1975) spanned the birth, growth, and maturity of city planning as a profession, and through his long and distinguished career, Stein helped to shape it. Yet he was known for his modesty about his own abilities and willingness to subsume his individual ambitions to the success of collaborative endeavors. As remembered by his colleague Lewis Mumford, Stein's "special facility was to evaluate important ideas, to choose congenial associates, seize imaginatively on their special talents and put them to work on tasks of research or design or construction that drew forth their best qualities. . . . An excellent judge of ideas, [he] was quite as keen a judge of men."[10]

Born in Rochester, New York, Stein moved at age eight with his family to New York City, where he attended the Ethical Culture Society's Workingman's School and received a

Figure 1.5.
Clarence S. Stein

progressive education that sought to stimulate his visual imagination and sense of social responsibility as well as his intellect.[11] After graduation and an unsatisfying two-year stint in his father's business, Stein briefly attended Columbia University's school of architecture with the intention of becoming an interior decorator, but left in 1903 to work in a decorator's studio in Paris. There, he shifted his career ambitions to "community architecture" and enrolled in the École des Beaux-Arts, from which he returned, as Mumford observed, educated in the Beaux Arts method but not tethered to classical clichés.[12] While in Paris, he absorbed a lasting impression of that city's urbanity and the way its buildings and streetscapes fit among and around well-designed, well-used green spaces. He also took a study trip to England, where he was stirred by the British town of Bournville, built by industrialist George Cadbury as a model village for the workers in his chocolate factory outside Birmingham.[13]

Back in New York in 1911, Stein began his architectural career in the office of Bertram Grosvenor Goodhue and in time advanced to chief designer. Among the projects Stein worked on during this period were the San Diego Exposition of 1915, St. Bartholomew's Church on Park Avenue in New York City, and the planned mining town of Tyrone, New Mexico, sponsored by the Phelps Dodge Company. The latter project, in particular, engaged him in addressing the issues inherent in planning a complex, large-scale environment.[14] During World War I, Stein served as a first lieutenant in the Army Corps of Engineers, and upon completion of his service in 1919 he set up his own architectural practice in association with Robert D. Kohn—a fellow housing reformer and member of the Ethical Culture Society—and Charles Butler, another alumnus of the École des Beaux-Arts who had worked with Kohn on the design of defense housing projects during World War I.

During the period between his return from Europe and 1920, Stein began to merge his ambitions as an architect with a growing commitment to social reform and public service, especially an interest in improving living conditions in the inner city. Most large American cities in the early twentieth century strove to increase their populations and thus their source of industrial productivity. The cities often made little or no corresponding effort to provide decent housing, education, and recreation for these workers, and so poverty, juvenile delinquency, crime, disease, and high mortality rates plagued urban tenements. Stein objected to the human costs of economic exploitation and advocated public responsibility to provide sufficient, well-lit, well-ventilated, sanitary dwellings.[15] He came to see clearly, in his own words, "the distinction between building for people or building for profit."[16]

Stein served from 1915 to 1919 as secretary of the City Planning Committee of the City Club, a civic betterment association in New York. In 1919 he joined the Hudson Guild, a West Side social settlement that brought him close to the problems of the urban poor and was influential in directing his professional interests to "social architecture." In the same year, Stein became secretary of the Housing Committee of the New York State Reconstruction Commission, formed to deal with the postwar housing shortage by promoting a long-term program of state involvement in providing comfortable dwellings for lower-income citizens. The housing crisis had also awakened an urgent awareness of housing and planning issues among the members of the American Institute of Architects (AIA), and in 1921 that group appointed Stein secretary of its newly formed Committee on Community Planning (CCP-AIA).

These affiliations familiarized Stein with the specific problems of urban shelter and provided him with the support and collaboration of an emerging group of intellectual architects, planners, economists, and civic leaders who shared his views on the social importance of good housing and comprehensive planning.

Stein formed the RPAA in order to enlist his friends and associates—many of them alumni of the federal government's short-lived World War I defense housing agencies—to help carry out the community planning program of the CCP-AIA. As recalled by RPAA charter member Mumford, "Almost overnight, Clarence Stein assembled a group dedicated not just to improving housing, but to acquiring the historic background and practical experience needed to make a fresh start in the whole area of city development."[17] Recognizing that new technology had the potential to transform entire patterns of living and to restructure people's relationships with one another, with cities, and with nature, the group studied and created models for twentieth-century city and regional development and organization.[18] Most contemporary architects focused on the design of individual structures (increasingly in the style of the European Modernists), and planning professionals tinkered with rudimentary zoning and building codes (often without a comprehensive plan), but the

RPAA focused on understanding and addressing broader patterns of urban and regional development.[19]

The RPAA's town and neighborhood planning schemes were heavily indebted to the utopian garden city ideals promulgated by Ebenezer Howard and his disciple, Raymond Unwin, at the end of the Victorian era, and its regional planning ideas were influenced by the ecological planning theories of Scottish biologist and planner Patrick Geddes. The RPAA's members, however, also held a fervent belief in the power of twentieth-century technologies such as the automobile, the telephone, and "Giant Power"—the new electrical power grid—to disperse population into small, self-contained, decentralized "regional cities," surrounded by agricultural land and connected by limited-access highways. Comprehensive planning toward this goal, they contended, would end the exploitation of rural land by the congested industrial metropolis, and ultimately lead to a widespread balance of population, resources, and institutions. In trying to address the pathologies of what they saw as an obsolete urban form, and in trying to forge an alternative to the cookie-cutter suburbia even then burgeoning on the city's edge, Stein and his colleagues created plans for inwardly focused communities they called New Towns, where pedestrians could find beauty, community with neighbors, and safety in interior garden courtyards, away from cars, which were relegated to perimeter roads. It was a radical vision of not only physical transformation but of economic redistribution.[20]

The intellectual power and influence of the RPAA was out of proportion to the size of its membership. With no more than more than twenty members at its peak, the organization never outgrew its intimate, salon-like character. It had no official mailing list, paid staff, or office space. Yet its gatherings, which occurred most often over lunch in New York's City Club and, later, in Clarence Stein's living room, brought together many of the most visionary social planners, architects, urbanists, and critics of the era. Aside from Stein and Mumford, whose verbal acumen placed him in the role of the group's public spokesman, the original members included Stein's new associate, Henry Wright; fellow architect-planners Frederick Bigger, Frederick Ackerman, Robert D. Kohn, and John Irwin Bright; conservationist and forester Benton MacKaye, designer of the Appalachian Trail; Charles Harris Whitaker, editor of the *Journal of the American Institute of Architects*; economist Stuart Chase; and real estate developer and former Ethical Culture School classmate of Stein's, Alexander Bing. Housing reformers who allied themselves with the RPAA included those, such as Bing, who promoted solutions from within a reorganized, reoriented private sector, and others, such as Catherine Bauer and Edith Elmer Wood, who advocated for public housing as a remedy to the intractable problems of private sector greed and chaos. Later members of the group included city planners Tracy Augur (who would later design the New Town of Norris, Tennessee, for the Tennessee Valley Authority), Russell Van Nest Black, Robert Bruere, Joseph K. Hart, and Clarence Perry, who first articulated the concept of the neighborhood unit as a building block of town and city planning. Together, the members of the RPAA sought to synthesize physical and social planning in a single integrated discipline.

Though their typical housing scheme was communitarian, with attached dwellings grouped around shared open space, the RPAA was not economically radical to the point of communism, nor were is members typical 1920s free marketeers. Stuart Chase referred to the group as "mildly socialistic," while Carl Sussman, who anthologized the writings of members of the RPAA in his book *Planning the Fourth Migration*, noted that they were "willing to abandon large areas of the free market in favor of a planned economy."[21] These attitudes were evidenced in the 1926 report to the New York state governor and legislature from the New York State Commission of Housing and Regional Planning, chaired by Stein and formulated with substantial contributions by Wright, Mum-

ford, and MacKaye. Having already recommended state au-
thorization of taxpayer-supported regional planning boards,
Stein's commission now advocated the development of a
statewide plan for the development of decentralized cities
amid natural areas set aside for conservation, recreation, or
agriculture.[22] This was a bold, far-sighted vision for a fundamental restructuring of the business of development, and to
build toward it would have required extensive public intervention in the private market. In the booming business climate
of the 1920s, the report was admired—and quietly filed.[23] In-
tellectually formidable as the RPAA alliance was, the prevailing political culture was more powerful still.

The RPAA was ambitious, but also short-lived. Historians have attributed its demise within a decade of its
founding to a number of causes, including its members' lack
of influence over the programs of the New Deal, a scattering
of their homes and jobs, competing professional interests,
and the inability of the New York inner circle to motivate
its members in other cities to establish regional chapters.[24]
While it lasted, however, this loose affiliation of urban
intellectuals exercised a persuasive voice in defining and
promoting the nascent field of city and regional planning.
For Stein, his relationships with fellow members of the
RPAA strongly influenced the types of projects he took on,
how he chose to handle them, and whom he selected as his
collaborators.

Throughout the 1920s, Stein's work expressed the RPAA's
emerging planning principles, especially in projects developed
with Henry Wright in New York and New Jersey (detailed in
chapter 2). By the start of the 1930s, Stein appeared to be professionally on the rise, but the New Deal's broad commitment
to the very policies Stein had been foremost in advocating—
regional planning, comprehensive community planning, and
quality subsidized housing for lower-income citizens—actually thwarted his career. Although Stein very much wanted
and actively sought a position as designer of one of the New

Deal Resettlement Administration's greenbelt towns, initiated in 1935 to rehouse low-income families in master-planned suburban communities, he was ultimately retained as a consultant and design reviewer while less experienced, less visionary planners actually implemented the new federal housing and planning programs. Perhaps he was passed over because he was unwilling to relocate to Washington, D.C., preferring to continue to work out of his New York City studio, or perhaps it was because he resisted the International Style architectural vocabulary which increasingly determined the form of large-scale multiunit housing. Like so many other architects during the Depression, Stein found he did not have enough commissions to sustain his practice.[25]

From 1935 on, Stein periodically withdrew from life and work into clinical depression, though he enjoyed significant periods of productivity with each recovery and return to professional activity. In the late 1930s, he addressed the functions and purposes of art museums after receiving a commission to design one in Wichita, Kansas; he collaborated with Lewis Mumford and Norman Bel Geddes on the classic film *The City;* and he attempted to revive the RPAA under the new title Council for Regional Development. In 1941, he served as consulting architect on Baldwin Hills Village, a planned community in Los Angeles. A decade later, MIT Press published Stein's book *Toward New Towns for America,* in which he set forth his evolving community planning theories through case studies of his previous projects. The book came out in the same year that Stein was selected from a competitive field of applicants to take on one more large-scale planning commission: designing the New Town of Kitimat, located in the wilderness of British Columbia near the smelter operations of the Aluminum Company of Canada. In 1956, Stein was awarded the gold medal by the AIA for his life's work. Mumford has written: "In a way, the 1950s corresponded to the 1920s in Stein's life. If the '20s was the seedtime of his planning ideas, the '50s was a belated harvest, partly nipped by

Figure 1.6. Henry Wright

frost, but with bright mellow fruit still left."[26] But the trajectory of Stein's career, like that of many other promising professionals, was interrupted by the Depression, and from this he never quite recovered. When he died in 1975 at the age of ninety-two, he was, in the words of *New York Times* architecture critic Ada Louise Huxtable, a forgotten prophet.[27]

Stein's closest collaborator was Henry Wright (1878–1936), himself a gifted planner, problem-solver, and housing reformer.[28] Stein described Wright as original and almost manic in his brilliance: "His reasoning was his own. . . . His was an unusually active mind—an inquisitive, analytical mind—that constantly drove him on from one problem to another, and from one solution to a still better solution of a problem."[29]

Wright received his bachelor's degree in architecture

from the University of Pennsylvania in 1901 but found his
calling in the practice of city planning, which was then
emerging out of landscape architecture as a distinct discipline. By 1903, Wright was developing parks in Kansas City.
He worked as a landscape designer for the St. Louis Fair, and
was active in the early city planning movement in the Mid-
west. In 1909, Wright established a landscape architecture
practice while organizing and serving as secretary of the
St. Louis City Plan Association.

During his time in St. Louis, Wright began to hone his
site-planning skills on several small subdivisions. Trained
and skilled in both architecture and landscape design, Wright
found subdivision planning a natural arena. His first efforts
were conventional neighborhoods of single-family homes
for the well-to-do. As rising land, finance, and building costs
put detached homes out of reach of many middle-class and
working families, however, Wright came to wrestle with a
more complex set of issues. He began to search for ways to
apply site design to the problems of housing economics, and
in so doing, stepped to the fore of a revolution in residential
planning that has influenced subdivision schemes to the
present day.

Through the end of the nineteenth century, with a few
upper-class exceptions such as Olmsted's Riverside (see chapter 2), designing a subdivision was in most cases a small-scale,
speculative endeavor. The process consisted simply of divid-
ing a parcel of land into the maximum number of buildable
lots and then either constructing houses on them or selling
the lots to someone who would. Motivated by profit, speculative developers favored efficient grid plans and seldom took
into consideration such factors as the relationship of the
house to the natural features of its site, to its neighbors, to
community services such as schools and shops, and to the
economics of supplying utilities and infrastructure—features
that make the difference between repetitive rows of housing
shells and a fully functional community.

Conscious of wasted space and expense, Wright began to design new subdivisions on the premise that each individual dwelling was necessarily connected, in numerous physical, economic, and social ways, to other dwellings and to the community as a whole. In St. Louis, he experimented with alternative ways of subdividing lots according to comprehensive community plans in which land, homes, transportation, services, and infrastructure were all considerations from the outset.

During World War I, Wright worked as a town planner for the Housing Division of the Emergency Fleet Corporation, the nation's first experiment with federally built housing. Afterward, he focused his attentions on better urban living. He was concerned not only with the familiar problem of slums but also with what he termed the "far more costly community pattern" of subdivision sprawl.[30] Through analysis of economics and space, Wright believed, this wasteful mode of building could be replaced with one that housed all classes of people efficiently, affordably, and attractively.

In 1923, Wright returned to New York to become the town planning consultant to the City Housing Corporation, the limited-dividend developer of garden city–inspired communities headed by his friend Alexander Bing. He also became involved with the CCP-AIA, and it was through this affiliation that he met Clarence Stein, who later remembered: "By working together we found that we were interested in the same objectives, although we had quite different contributions to make in their attainment. We found that we [both] could not fit our conceptions into the pattern of the existing city, its manner of physical growth and the economic or social methods of bringing about that growth."[31] Like Stein, Wright held the goal of designing "adequate shelter in a desirable environment—to replace slums, rehabilitate blighted areas, and develop new neighborhoods as actually needed. Intended for those of lowest incomes, as a public responsibility; for clerical workers, as more suitably located than outer sub-

urbs; for young well-to-do families, as better than usual speculative houses or apartments."[32]

The personal and professional relationship Stein and
Wright forged lasted through the early 1930s. In 1923, Wright
cofounded the RPAA with Stein, and in 1925, he succeeded
Stein as secretary of the CCP-AIA.

During the early 1930s, Wright's continuing passion for
community design led him to immerse himself in the study
of European Modernist developments. He became an advocate of "group housing," or row houses, in place of large apartment blocks, and avidly studied the costs and benefits of hillside housing development.[33] Wright considered himself a
planner and economic analyst, not an architect, and was
quick to accept Modernism as a design paradigm without regard for its social or aesthetic meanings. His primary interest
was in cost ratios of housing to land and roads and in the orientation of rooms within dwellings in the tradition of philanthropic housing. In 1933, Wright, Lewis Mumford, and architect Albert Mayer founded the Housing Study Guild, which
trained young architects in Wright's approach to cost analysis
and planning.[34] In 1935, Wright joined the Faculty of Town
Planning in the Architecture School at Columbia University,
and published a book, *Rehousing Urban America*, based on his
observations of European housing and application of them to
American circumstances.

Wright's attitude toward the economic rations of housing
to site influenced Stein's quest to develop affordable housing
through innovative land use schemes. However, ideological
differences and problems working together caused Stein and
Wright to end their partnership in 1933. In that year, Stein
wrote to his wife, Aline:

Henry and I had a talk yesterday as to our future relations. . . . It has
been growing more and more apparent to me that the relation of
partners in any of these jobs is difficult. . . . In fact, in any housing
problem where there are so many possible solutions and so many
factors to be considered, a time comes when someone must decide

on the road to take, and then stick to it. . . . Henry, as you know, is not one to cooperate on final decisions or to take the responsibility of action. On the other hand, he is an inspiring (if sometimes annoying) critic. Hereafter he is to be consultant on my work as on that of other architects.[35]

Stein and Wright had reached an intellectual impasse. Wright was increasingly in the thrall of the European Modernists—in 1934, his Housing Study Guild concluded that high-rise towers were, after all, the most economical urban housing form—while Stein rejected the "towers in the park" approach, continuing to promote, instead, urban decentralization into low-rise New Towns.[36] Architecturally, Stein was steeped in the traditions of the École des Beaux-Arts and the English garden city, and had little use for the stark Modernist aesthetic.[37] The difference was fundamental, and Chatham Village was the last project on which the two men collaborated as partners, although Stein maintained respect for Wright through the end of his life.

The third Buhl Foundation consultant to significantly influence Chatham Village was Frederick Bigger (1881–1963), a respected Pittsburgh architect, city planner, and public servant noted for his frank, impartial judgments and sound business sense.[38] Bigger epitomized the rational planner of the early twentieth century. He believed that city life could be perfected through efficient, comprehensive administrative control of subdivisions, streets, and buildings. More broadly, he strove to rise above fractious politics and a piecemeal approach to planning and to establish the role of municipal government in comprehensive planning for livable urban environments.[39]

Bigger attended the University of Pennsylvania with Henry Wright and graduated in 1903. His early architecture practice in Philadelphia and Seattle occurred during the peak years of city planning as informed by the Progressive and City Beautiful movements, and Bigger internalized the philosophies of both. In 1913, Bigger returned to his native Pittsburgh to espouse the value of well-planned playgrounds, park systems, boulevards, and civic beauty.

Like other early twentieth-century reformers, Bigger believed that corrupt city politicians and merciless capitalism were to blame for the blight, congestion, and social inequity that plagued his city. Yet unlike many adherents of City Beautiful planning, Bigger understood that an attractive, healthy urban environment would not follow from aesthetic dressing up alone, but rather from the integration of architectural improvements into a broader scope of useful social, economic, and physical planning initiatives.[40] From 1913 to 1918, when he worked as assistant secretary to the newly organized Pittsburgh Art Commission, Bigger matured from a follower of the City Beautiful into a leading advocate for comprehensive planning.

A self-described architect and town planner, Bigger entered the national discourse on city and regional planning during World War I. Like Clarence Stein and Henry Wright, Bigger served as secretary of the CCP-AIA, a position that brought him to the center of the national discussion of urban blight, slum clearance, and low-income housing. In 1918 he cofounded, with a number of prominent Pittsburgh citizens including Henry Buhl, the Citizens' Committee on the City Plan (CCCP), whose mission was nothing less than to create a comprehensive, scientifically ordered city plan for Pittsburgh in which residence, recreation, transportation, and industry would all be linked in a healthy, attractive, efficiently functioning city.

Bigger's ideal was an integrated "metropolitan district," in which urban chaos would be conquered by means of wide, well-located streets; affordable, attractive housing; extensive park systems; strategically located playgrounds, efficient transit; and up-to-date infrastructure. Pittsburgh's topography, fragmented by rivers, valleys, hills, and ravines, presented particular challenges, and this discontinuity of the physical environment tended to create, in turn, ethnic and class divi-

Figure 1.7. Frederick Bigger

sions by which "inferior politicians played off one district against another."[41] In Bigger's vision, comprehensive planning would restore physical and social connections, bringing order to Pittsburgh's haphazardly built urban environment and up-lifting the circumstances of its citizens.

In 1922, Pittsburgh mayor William Magee appointed Bigger to the Pittsburgh City Planning Commission, whose membership, not coincidentally, had considerable overlap with that of the CCCP. The two organizations had generally the same goal: to promote the conformance of land use in Pittsburgh to that prescribed by a comprehensive plan. In 1934, Bigger assumed the chair of the commission and held that position until his retirement in 1954. For twenty years,

Bigger's commitment to an uncrowded, unblighted, socially inclusive, and democratically accessible Pittsburgh guided the planning decisions that shaped the city.

Bigger found like-minded planners among the members of the RPAA. His friendships and correspondence with Lewis Mumford, Russell Van Nest Black, and, especially, neighborhood planner Clarence Perry were influential in expanding the social perspective of his 1923 Pittsburgh Parks plan, in which Bigger envisioned groupings of parks, playgrounds, and civic buildings such as schools and libraries forming true community centers for neighborhoods. And Bigger took a significant and lifelong interest in Chatham Village, where Clarence Stein and Henry Wright applied RPAA planning principles to one of the city's most challenging building sites.

This experience proved valuable when Bigger was appointed chief of planning for Roosevelt's greenbelt towns program. In this position, Bigger oversaw each local planning team and approved all plans, from large-scale site and housing schemes to detailed specifications for fixtures and plantings.[42] Bigger set forth broad objectives that were consistent with the ideas of the RPAA: each community should be whole unto itself, incorporating a greenbelt buffer, modest family housing, and careful attention to site planning and topography.[43]

In 1937, Bigger left his chief of planning post. He continued to serve as chair of the Pittsburgh City Planning Commission, even as he spent much of his time in Washington, D.C. As the federal government's focus shifted in the late 1930s to the redevelopment of blighted inner-city areas, Bigger helped to shape federal policy on urban renewal. In 1941, when the Federal Housing Administration (FHA) published *A Handbook on Urban Redevelopment for Cities in the United States,* Deputy Commissioner Earle S. Draper gave Bigger the major credit for its authorship. The FHA's goal was to help older cities that had deteriorated due to years of neglect during the

Depression understand their problems in preparation for making large-scale, postwar redevelopment plans. Drawing on Bigger's longtime planning agenda in Pittsburgh, the handbook emphasized the necessity of government-initiated planning on a comprehensive scale to achieve healthily functioning communities.[44] In 1948, Bigger accepted an appointment by President Truman to the National Capital Planning Commission and became involved in urban renewal planning for southwest Washington, D.C.

Bigger's decades of public service at the local and federal levels laid much of the groundwork for the Pittsburgh Renaissance, but under Mayor David Lawrence, a new power structure emerged, and the city's Urban Redevelopment Authority assumed control of planning for the Pittsburgh Renaissance. Thus Bigger found himself at the margins of local planning at the moment when the city finally embraced his long-held ideals. Bigger lived out most of his years in a book-filled apartment in Chatham Village.[45]

The men behind Chatham Village personified divergent perspectives in community planning that took hold in the United States after World War I. The war had ushered in an era of rational planning marked by a faith in modern technology to create a new urban order. Stein, Wright, and Bigger shared a critique of capitalism that attributed most, if not all, urban ills to deliberate policies of economic exploitation. Their solution, the provision of livable environments through comprehensive public planning, was institutionalized by Franklin D. Roosevelt in the New Deal and has continued to influence urban and suburban development patterns. The three architect-planners had a point: economic opportunism had bred intolerable physical and social pathologies in Pittsburgh and other late-industrial cities. But Charles Lewis, though he saw clearly that poorly planned, indifferently implemented development was the source of many of the problems plaguing urban housing, detested the thought of reform rooted in state control. He fervently believed the solution should come from within the private building industry. Lewis believed that capitalism should not be regulated, but enlightened.

Although Lewis and his city planning consultants represented different viewpoints on the nature of the urban housing crisis, they converged in their thoughts on a solution. New communities, planned and built from the ground up, using model, modern principles of design and democratic order, would demonstrate how all Americans could participate in a better pattern of living.

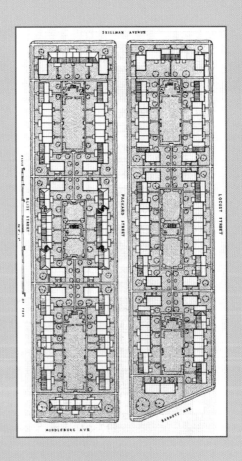

two Precedent and Process

Chatham Village has its antecedents in the garden city movement, instigated by Ebenezer Howard at end of the nineteenth century. A parliamentary clerk in London, then the world's largest city, Howard saw all around him the pathological consequences of the Industrial Revolution. Lured by comparatively high wages, people streamed to the city in search of factory jobs, but urban pollution and high costs kept them living in cramped and crowded slums. Britain's nineteenth-century industrialized cities juxtaposed the squalor of the laboring classes alongside the opulence of the elite. Howard observed firsthand how cities abounded with opportunities for jobs, culture, and social interaction, but also removed working people completely from wholesome contact with nature and presented instead a congested, filthy, and toxic environment.

Influenced by his reading of reformist literature—including *Looking Backward*, Edward Bellamy's 1888 novel about a socialist utopia, and *Hygeia, or the City of Health*, an 1876 pamphlet by Dr. Benjamin Ward Richardson that described a low-density city with wide streets, an underground railway, and abundant parks[1]—Howard envisioned a more egalitarian community that would enable people to live balanced lives with "all the advantages of the most energetic and active town, all the beauty and delight of the country." In 1898, he published a book called *To-morrow: A Peaceful Path to Real Reform*, describing and diagramming how to build and live in his ideal "garden city." The book sold briskly, and in 1902 Howard slightly revised it for reissue under the title *Garden Cities of To-morrow*.[2]

The garden city Howard depicted was a self-sufficient community of thirty thousand people to be built from scratch on a six-thousand-acre plot of rural land. Each garden city would be limited in size by its ability to supply all necessary basic services while still maintaining accessibility of people to commerce, work, and recreation, as well as facilitating convenient communication among the residents.[3] High-speed rail would connect communities of this type dispersed across a regional network, and although there was to be a central city, Howard envisioned them all coexisting as "social cities" that would achieve a more democratic distribution of wealth, culture, and industry than the traditional metropolitan area hierarchy.

At the core of each garden city was a five-and-a-half-acre central park, surrounded by civic, cultural, and medical buildings. Another 145-acre park encircled those structures. The

Crystal Palace, a glass-enclosed shopping arcade, created a
link between the public open space and the residential ring of
the town. In six wards, concentric tree-lined streets connected by radial boulevards provided access to homes,
schools, and gardens. The garden city was a pedestrian community in which no house was more than six hundred yards
from the community's center.

Industry was relegated to the outer edges of the circular
city. Here factories, warehouses, and coal and timber yards
faced outward onto an orbital railway that encompassed the
town and delivered goods to and from its people and businesses. Outside of the industrial belt was a five-thousand-acre
swath of agricultural land that, in Howard's scheme, would be

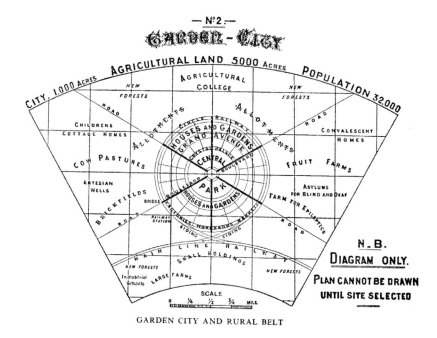

Figure 2.1. General schematic diagram of Ebenezer Howard's garden city
concept, c. 1898

home to an additional two thousand people engaged in farming. This permanent greenbelt would provide food for the city, prevent its expansion beyond the planned optimum size, and insulate it against potentially damaging outside forces.

Howard's was a holistic vision for integrating the interests of the individual and the community. As such, it extended beyond physical planning to embrace property ownership. Aware that the financial structure of the garden city would have lasting consequences for its built environment, Howard suggested a cooperative arrangement whereby the residents would be neither tenants nor owners of discrete individual properties, but trustees with a financial as well as a social stake in the whole community. Land would be purchased at agricultural value, and the increase in its value would be returned to the community to the benefit of all who lived there. A reform-minded planner who idealized a decentralized, cooperative society, Howard sought a system that would encourage working people to invest in cooperative enterprises as an alternative to paying speculative builders.[4]

Developed as a theory, not a blueprint, Howard's prototype was rather simplistic and diagrammatic. Only two garden cities were ever built directly according to its precepts: Letchworth and Welwyn, both in England. A third English community, Hampstead Garden Suburb, demonstrated the applicability of low-density garden city principles to suburban development and marked the beginning of a lasting tradition of garden suburb planning.

Beyond these limited demonstrations, the ideas behind the garden city model were widely disseminated, and Howard's attitudes toward land, density, self-sufficiency, and zoning became a fundamental principle of community planning.

As Howard was formulating his diagrams in England, Progressive-era reformers were taking a regulatory approach to improving conditions in America's urban tenements. New zoning and building codes offered the means to legislate minimum standards of public health and safety, but even with more fire escapes, windows, and bathrooms, cities remained crowded, unsanitary, and inhospitable places for a great many residents. As public housing advocate and RPAA member Edith Elmer Wood stated, restrictive building legislation "may forbid the bad house, but it does not provide the good one."[5]

Many urban reformers shared Wood's view that legislation in this arena was proving ineffective. An illustration in Catherine Bauer's classic 1934 book, *Modern Housing*, shows a city neighborhood of bleak, monotonous, walk-up tenements, relieved only by the swags of laundry hanging across the alley and the litter strewn on the pavement. The absence of trees, grass, or even weeds suggests the harshness of such an environment for human habitation. The caption reads, "New Law tenements in New York, the result of arduous 'reform.' *Only the luckiest third could pay for* [*this*]" (italics original).[6] In this climate of weak legislative reform, American architects, planners, and housing reformers seized Ebenezer Howard's garden city theories and applied them to their own search for more fundamental remedies to the blighted, burgeoning industrial metropolis and, increasingly, the haphazard spread of speculative suburbs. The American garden city emerged not only from Howard's theories and its early implementations, but from a rich American tradition of striving toward balance between the individual and the community; the urban and the rural; and connection with fellow citizens and oneness with nature.

Various communities claim to be the first garden city in America. Predating Howard's book by thirty years, the Chicago suburb of Riverside, Illinois, designed by Frederick Law Olmsted Sr., established the concept of setting a middle-class residential area within a carefully designed landscape using nature, not streets and buildings, as the focal point. The public open spaces and pleasant promenades at Riverside were meant, as in a garden city, to facilitate a sense of community and civic participation. A parkway, planned to connect Riverside to Chicago but never built, would have provided separate

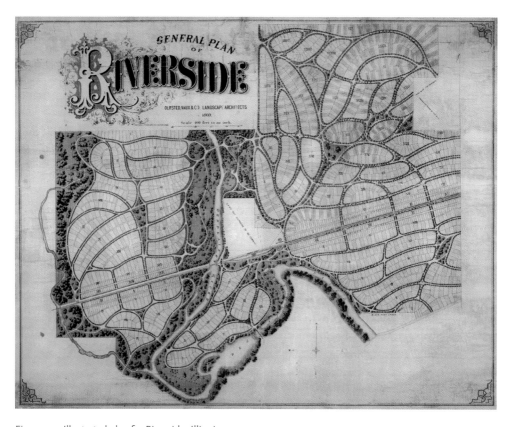

Figure 2.2. Illustrated plan for Riverside, Illinois

lanes for carriages, riders on horseback, and pedestrians. In the roads through Olmsted's Central Park in New York, this idea was realized, complete with over- and underpasses to avoid dangerous intersections. Stein acknowledged that Olmsted's approach provided an important precedent to the systems of pedestrian and vehicular separation that he and Wright later pioneered at in Radburn, New Jersey, and Chatham Village.[7]

Roland Park, an upper-class neighborhood of Baltimore developed between 1890 and 1920 by Edward Bouton and planned in part by Frederick Law Olmsted Jr., included a winding street pattern that responded to the area's natural topography and uniform house, lot, and setback sizes. The community utilized restrictive deed covenants to protect the integrity of the designed landscapes and architecture and incorporated one of the country's first shopping centers—a single building containing six stores that opened in 1907.[8] Further innovations included a separate maintenance corporation to which each resident contributed an annual assessment and a board of architectural review to assure that new building plans were consonant with the community's prevailing aesthetic. Although Roland Park featured some of the most attractive qualities of Howard's garden city idea, and took tentative steps toward establishing communal investment in and responsibility for shared amenities, it lacked other, fundamental garden city features, such as any industrial or agricultural land. In its uniform emphasis on large, single-family homes, Roland Park, like Riverside, lacked the progressive, reformist underpinnings of later American garden city experiments that sought to make the spaciousness and comfort of suburban life accessible to those who could not typically afford it.

Bouton and Olmsted Jr. also participated in the planning, development, and design of Forest Hills Gardens, a streetcar suburb initiated in 1908 in Queens, New York. Like Chatham Village, Forest Hills Gardens was founded by a philanthropic organization—in this case, the Russell Sage Foundation—to demonstrate the practicality and profitability of good design and comprehensive planning.[9] Also like Chatham Village, Forest Hills Gardens embraced standardization, technology, and efficiencies of scale in order to control construction costs. Olmsted collaborated on the community's modified grid plan and eclectic, English-inspired aesthetic with Grosvenor Atterbury, an architect known primarily for his work on lavish houses for wealthy industrialists. Atterbury, who evinced a keen interest in model housing and building technology, developed an innovative, protomodern construction method at Forest Hills Gardens in which each house was built from standardized, precast panels that were fabricated off-site, embedded with electrical wiring, and assembled by crane. The savings in construction costs furthered the Sage Foundation's goal of keeping housing costs down (although, ultimately, the Sage Foundation lost money on the venture). Forest Hills Gardens was built intentionally as a middle-class suburb, and so, like Roland Park, became more of a bedroom community than a full-fledged garden city. However, in its association with progressive philanthropy, its purpose in demonstrating the superiority of large-scale capitalization and planning over typical speculative development, its provision of common open spaces, and the modern technology applied to achieving its unified, romantic appearance, Forest Hills Gardens is an important precursor to the development of Chatham Village.

In 1921, landscape architect John Nolen—who had studied under Frederick Law Olmsted Jr. at Harvard and was a close personal friend of Raymond Unwin's—designed the garden suburb of Mariemont outside Cincinnati, Ohio. Mariemont was underwritten by Mary Emery, a wealthy widow, who financed the planned community as a place where Cincinnati's workers could escape living in slums. Nolen viewed this as an opportunity to design a "national exemplar" and included a mix of row, semidetached, and detached housing to serve families of all incomes. Despite this intention, the suburb,

Figure 2.3. Forest Hills Gardens, New York

Figure 2.4. Rendering of residential lane and cul-de-sac in Mariemont, Ohio

like Roland Park and Forest Hills Gardens, ended up serving mainly the middle class.

Mariemont's "town centre" encompassed a village green, service and retail businesses, an open-air market, an inn, a town hall, a fire station, and civic offices. Residential neighborhoods were zoned by size and class of housing, and some streets were laid out to follow the natural contours of the site. Nolen dispersed church and school sites throughout, included ample adjacent parkland, and separated land zoned for industrial development below a bluff. A hospital, model farm, and planned (but never completed) museum of Native American artifacts rounded out the community.

Mariemont was a comprehensive and thoughtful, if not slavish, adaptation of Howard's garden city ideas to an American metropolitan suburb. Lacking a greenbelt, however, Mariemont became one of many contiguous suburban places—albeit one distinguished by its picturesque street- and landscapes—rather than a garden city in the sense that Howard had intended.[10]

As garden city ideas gained currency among American planners, a growing contingent of American housing reform activists began to embrace the movement's goals of ending suburban sprawl through the creation of self-sufficient New Towns, making housing affordable through nonspeculative forms of real estate ownership, and incorporating communal amenities within walking distance of homes. These "housers," including RPAA members Catherine Bauer and Edith Elmer Wood, looked to Europe for models not just of what new residential communities would look like, but also for and by whom they would be built. Housers doubted the significance of isolated experiments such as Forest Hills Gardens or Mariemont; in fact, they rejected outright the notion that either private enterprise or charity could succeed at creating ideal residential communities on the scale necessary to revolutionize American housing. The uncoordinated activity and unbridled greed of private enterprise had created the problem of inadequate and overpriced housing in the first place, while "philanthropy has had from the beginning of time until now to solve the problem of housing the poor," Wood told a U.S. Senate subcommittee in 1911, "and it has never done so in any place at any time."[11] Wood, Bauer, and their cohorts advocated for an active government role in the provision of comprehensively planned communities, not only for the poorest citizens who could not afford adequate shelter without assistance, but for the working- and middle-class families who constituted the majority of the population.

Due to the tireless crusading of Bauer, in particular, a permanent American public housing program would, indeed, be established in 1937. But during the first third of the twentieth century, the very idea of public housing faced formidable opposition from the construction industry and from political conservatives, whose supply-side economic policies fueled the Roaring Twenties. Housers saw a brief window of opportunity during World War I, when the federal government entered the housing sector to address the emergency shortage of housing for defense workers. Two federal agencies, the Emergency Fleet Corporation and the United States Housing Corporation, built temporary housing for single male laborers and permanent residential communities for families during 1917 and 1918. In his capacity as head architect of the Emergency Fleet Corporation's Division of Housing, Robert Kohn (Clarence Stein's associate) guided the design of large-scale communities in which parks and social spaces were planned as instruments of nurturing a more cohesive and democratic society.[12] At war's end, however, the finished communities were sold and the incomplete ones abandoned mid-construction as the programs that created them were truncated.

Public housing, which seemed an impossibly radical idea during the economic boom of the 1920s, appeared a more attainable goal in the political economy of the Great Depression, which was more open to experimentation, change, and,

most significantly, an increased role for government in providing services that the private sector would or could not. The
crisis of families turned out of their homes by foreclosure
also offered an opportunity for housing reformers of all
stripes to demonstrate alternatives to the traditional, speculatively built, owner-occupied, single-family dwelling. In 1933,
several of the RPAA's core members reconvened as the Housing Study Guild to advocate for a government housing program based on garden city and regional planning principles.
Instead of wasting time and money on slum clearance, the
guild called for the funding of public agencies, cooperatives,
and limited-dividend corporations to build comprehensively
planned garden city–inspired communities on inexpensive
land on urban peripheries. Once low-income populations had
been attracted to these green, modern New Towns, the guild's
theory held, inner-city slum conditions would gradually dis-
appear. The members of the Housing Study Guild did not all
agree, however, and the by the mid-1930s, Catherine Bauer
had distanced herself from the group, claiming that it sought
to "bestow" housing solutions from the top down, rather than
mobilizing workers on behalf of public housing.[13]

American experimentation with the marriage of planned
garden communities and publicly built housing culminated in
Roosevelt's greenbelt towns program. Roosevelt had attended
a meeting of the RPAA in Virginia in 1931, when he was still
governor of New York, where he heard Lewis Mumford, Benton MacKaye, and Stuart Chase speak about the importance
of regional planning and garden city principles. President
Roosevelt's Resettlement Administration, created in 1935 and
headed by Rexford G. Tugwell, envisioned a nationwide network of fifty experimental "satellite towns" in the mode of
the RPAA's regionally dispersed New Towns but ultimately
ended up planning only four and building only three—Greenbelt, Maryland; Green Hills, Ohio; and Greendale, Wisconsin—before succumbing to conservative opposition regarding
its allegedly socialist agenda. Like the World War I defense

housing communities, the greenbelt towns were sold after
the war, while America's public housing program became a
welfare program for the poor that retained only the most rudimentary trace of garden city planning ideals.

The development of garden city ideals in the private and
public arenas throughout the 1920s and 1930s influenced—and
were in turn influenced by—Clarence Stein and Henry
Wright. Stein and Wright were especially interested in the
ideas of Raymond Unwin, and in 1924 they traveled to England where they met Unwin and Ebenezer Howard and saw
firsthand the garden cities and suburbs Unwin helped to design. In Unwin's book *Town Planning in Practice* (1909), and
subsequent pamphlet, *Nothing Gained by Overcrowding* (1912),

Figure 2.5. Aerial view of Greenbelt, Maryland, 1937

he argued that lower building densities yielded as much as higher densities to the investor, and that streets represented the most expensive and least satisfactory form of open space imaginable. Since a small number of grouped buildings or attached units required fewer streets to provide frontage, therefore leaving more land open for parks, recreation areas, and gardens, Unwin advocated: "We must work on the principle of grouping our buildings and combining our open spaces, having areas fairly closely built upon, surrounded by others of open space, rather than that of scattering and indefinitely mixing our buildings and our spaces."[14]

Stein and Wright were not the first to apply Unwin's "garden apartment" concept to American cities, but their work illustrates the clearest lineage to Chatham Village in its focus on nature, not buildings, as the dominant presence on the land.[15] Their work was emphatically not a romantic movement, however; Stein and Wright embraced the potential of electricity, the telephone, and the automobile to bring about transformative social as well as physical change. "Our cities are obsolete," Stein declared in 1933, comparing industrialized cities to automobile factories—when Ford's plants no longer served to build his current model of car, Ford scrapped them and built anew. But "city developers try to patch the obsolete machines," Stein wrote. "As a result, the physical structure of our 19th century cities fits the needs of our 20th century life about as well as a covered wagon would serve the needs of a present day continental tourist."[16] Stein even went so far as to analyze the Depression in these terms. Awed by the pace of innovation at the start of the twentieth century, Stein wrote: "This so-called depression is probably merely the culmination of the most radical changes man has ever known. Technological development has completely changed the possibility of life." Stein felt that the Great Depression was a deeply significant transition period in a Social Darwinist progression from primitive to advanced civilization.[17]

Stein and his colleagues tried to plan for the lasting impacts that the Depression, together with technological advancement, would have on American ways of life. They saw that machine labor and new patterns of part-time employment would create more leisure time than Americans had known before. Stein wrote that the most important task facing architects was that of building "a richer and finer environment in which to enjoy the profit from our leisure" and even to make "unemployment a blessing instead of a curse." Such an environment could not be attained by the old, piecemeal, speculative method of development in which "sale, not use, was the basic purpose of plan and subdivision."[18] Technological advances had made large-scale planning and construction of whole communities possible and it was by this method, proclaimed Stein, Wright, and their colleagues, that the leisure cities for the twentieth century must be built.

In an article entitled "The Planned Community," published in April 1933, Stein and several fellow members of the RPAA, calling themselves the Committee on Housing Exhibition, summarized their philosophy and program of community building for the twentieth century:

The cause of our failure to improve the great mass of housing during the last generation is due to the fact that we have brought to the new situation in housing an antiquated set of methods, habits, and ideals. We have continued to think of the dwelling house as a free and independent unit like the old-fashioned farmhouse or suburban cottage of the Eighties: a unit to be designed by itself, to be financed by itself, to be built by itself, to have for itself sufficient land to the care of every need for sunlight and recreation. Meanwhile, the new utilities and conveniences of urban living have destroyed this kind of self-sufficiency; and the houses we build have all the disadvantages of an obsolete form and layout and none of the positive virtues of our new mode of community organization.

The modern dwelling house is a unit in a neighborhood community. To design a house that will accommodate all the needs of modern living, one must also design the community. To build such a community effectively and cheaply, one must do it, where possible, in a single operation from the purchase of the raw land to the final plan and construction of its shops, schools, playgrounds, and other communal facilities.[19]

The advantages of comprehensive community design were economic as well as social. In a planned community, the article stated, "every road can be built economically for the exact use that it is to serve instead of being wastefully planned so that it will fit all possible changes. . . . Good planning and large-scale construction can make savings enough through the elimination of unnecessary roads alone, to pay for parks and play spaces."[20] Stein concluded that anything less than the building of complete neighborhoods was "pure waste," for any piecemeal development would be obsolete long before its costs could be fully amortized.

In 1924, the same year as their trip to England, Stein and Wright had their first opportunity to test some of these tenets when they accepted a commission from their friend Alexander Bing at the City Housing Corporation to be the architects of Sunnyside Gardens, a prototypical garden community developed on 1,100 building lots in Long Island City (Queens), New York. Working within the extant city grid (borough authorities would not allow any existing streets to be vacated), Sunnyside demonstrated how conventional New York City blocks could provide dense, affordable, multifamily housing on the perimeters with oases of common green space inside. Easements placed on all deeds prevented property owners from converting the park-like block centers for private use. The buildings at Sunnyside housed 1,231 families at completion—slightly over one family per lot of the site as it was originally divided—and covered only 28 percent of the available land. The rest was devoted to communal courtyards, gardens, and landscaped grounds.

Sunnyside was built, Stein declared, as "a laboratory, an experiment, a voyage of discovery, and an adventure," and its success led Stein, Wright, and the City Housing Corporation to embark upon a far more ambitious venture in 1928. The sub-

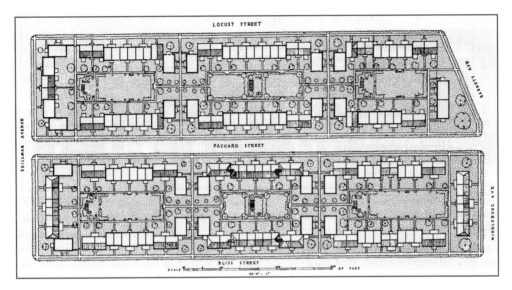

Figure 2.6. Partial plan of Sunnyside Gardens development, showing how Stein and Wright arranged attached living units around interior courtyards on standard New York City blocks.

Figure 2.7. The buildings of Sunnyside Gardens were designed by RPAA member Frederick Ackerman.

Figure 2.8. Through-block pathway at Sunnyside Gardens

urban New Town of Radburn, New Jersey, was an attempt to apply Howard's garden city principles and the lessons learned at Sunnyside to a fully planned American garden city for the modern motor age. In discussing their goals, Radburn's planners realized that a New Town in the twentieth-century United States must wrestle with a contemporary fact of life that British garden city planners had been spared thirty years before: the car. Therefore, Stein and Wright's design for Radburn merged Howard's garden city ideals with their own practical innovations for safe coexistence with the automobile. Stein and Wright pioneered the idea of planning for the integration of the automobile into residents' daily habits, even as they painstakingly separated vehicular roads from routes designed for pedestrians. Stein wrote that Radburn was designed to meet the "pressing need" of "a town in which people could live peacefully with the automobile—or rather in spite of it."[21]

As originally planned, the development was to occupy two square miles of former spinach fields in the rural borough of Fairlawn, New Jersey, sixteen miles away from Manhattan. Although they had worked successfully within the urban grid at Sunnyside, Stein believed "the flood of motors had already made the gridiron street pattern, which had formed the framework for urban real estate for over a century, as obsolete as a fortified town wall."[22] In Radburn, the borough did not yet have an official street plan or zoning ordinance, freeing Stein and Wright to experiment with their own ideas for road and building layout.

Radburn was to be a self-contained suburb, housing twenty-five thousand people in three neighborhoods. Designed to foster a rich family life, Radburn adopted the concept of the neighborhood unit as developed by RPAA member Clarence Perry. Perry's ideal neighborhood was defined by six essential elements: size, boundaries, open spaces, institutional sites, local commercial area, and an internal street system. The neighborhood unit was composed of four thousand to seven thousand people, or enough to support an elementary school, all living within comfortable walking distance (defined as one-half mile) of that school. Radburn's neighborhoods were thus conceived as three overlapping circles, each one mile in diameter, each served by an elementary school at its center and a shopping center. The community contained one high school, located at the site's highest point and center of the town.

Pedestrian walkways wound through parkland on the interiors of blocks, separated from vehicular roads on the perimeter. Roads were also arranged in a hierarchy to "unscramble the varied services of urban streets,"[23] with main through highways branching into smaller neighborhood access roads

Figure 2.9. General plan of Radburn, New Jersey, showing how its three neighborhoods were planned so that each family lived within one-half mile's walking distance of an elementary school.

Figure 2.10. Radburn's houses were oriented toward communal parkland.

and these, in turn, leading to smaller still cul-de-sac streets
that served fifteen to twenty houses each. A system of over-
passes and underpasses allowed pedestrians to traverse the
community without ever crossing a street surface. In keeping
with Unwin's ideal, only 21 percent of Radburn's land area was
road (as opposed to 35 percent in a conventionally designed
community), conserving money and space for parkland. The
cul-de-sacs were loosely based on those designed by Raymond
Unwin at Hampstead Garden Suburb; Unwin was in the
United States and in contact with Stein and Wright during
the fall of 1928.[24]

The planning principles Stein and Wright pioneered at
Radburn, including superblocks without through traffic, continuous parkland connecting the centers of blocks, a hier-

Figure 2.11. Walking paths through the interiors of Radburn's blocks separated pedestrian from vehicular movement.

archy of roads, and the complete separation of pedestrian and vehicular circulation routes, became known collectively as "The Radburn Idea." Most famous among these innovations was Radburn's reversal of the usual suburban street pattern. Instead of rows of evenly spaced houses, each centered in their individual yards and facing the streets which served them, Radburn pioneered the use of the suburban super-block—a large cluster of houses that turned away from the perimeter roadways and faced inward to communal lawns and gardens. Actually, each Radburn house had two faces. Its living areas faced inward toward pedestrian walkways and the park at the center of the block, while the kitchen and service areas faced the cul-de-sac, the street, and the connection to

Figure 2.12. This 1929 aerial view of Radburn shows clearly the relationships of buildings, parkland, and streets.

the highway. Radburn was "a town turned outside-in—without any backdoors."[25] Like the garden city idea itself, the Radburn houses attempted to reconcile the dual desires of city and country living.[26]

Radburn's first neighborhood was still being built when the stock market crashed in 1929, and, burdened with heavy upfront infrastructure costs, construction ground to a halt. Even incomplete, Radburn embodied the ideals of the RPAA: a safe, pleasant, uncrowded setting for suburban life made possible by affordable housing; ample open space; and integrated, comprehensive planning of the community's homes, highways, utilities, and services.

Stein and Wright's work at Sunnyside and Radburn constituted the prototype material for their third and final collaborative community, Chatham Village, but the idea for this Pittsburgh neighborhood had its practical beginnings with Charles Lewis. In 1929, with the housing market in Pittsburgh at a virtual standstill, Lewis saw the opportunity for the Buhl Foundation to invest not only in much-needed new dwellings, but in social change. He believed that the foundation's creation of a profitable and well-planned housing project would encourage others to support similar large-scale developments for people who had been foreclosed out of their pre-Depression homes. Lewis envisioned that expert designers would demonstrate how Pittsburgh's challenging terrain could be developed with economy of construction and beauty of form. But for all its high-minded purpose, Lewis's new community was to be no charitable venture. The limited-dividend project would generate revenue for the foundation, allowing it to increase its philanthropic activities, and demonstrating to other private investors that there was money to be made in housing a class of people they generally chose to overlook.

In order to convince the board of managers that investment in housing would be economically feasible, Lewis initiated a solid year of research, guided by the fact that, although the limited-dividend idea was untried in Pittsburgh, "in the few instances where commercial enterprise has been linked with social vision in other cities, . . . notable results have been achieved." Through interviews, published material, and field investigations, he studied the leading experiments in limited-dividend housing development, including the City Housing Corporation communities at Sunnyside and Radburn; the Rockefeller apartments in New York City; and the Julius Rosenwald Fund's Michigan Boulevard apartments in Chicago. In his report to the board of managers in spring of 1930, Lewis concluded, "it is commercially feasible to provide housing . . . for large groups that commercial builders do not now reach."[27]

Lewis also emphasized the importance of harnessing social vision to commercial enterprise, mentioning ominously

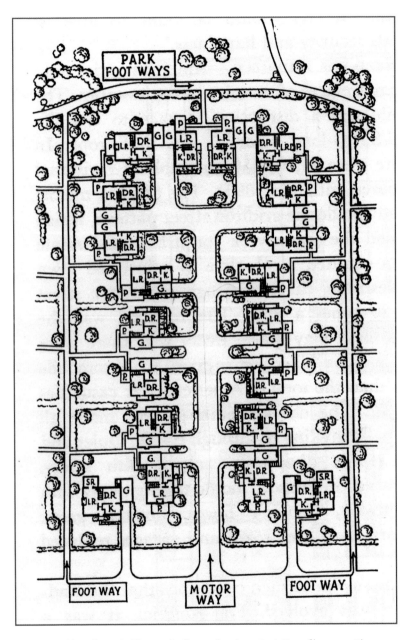

Figure 2.13. Plan of a typical lane at Radburn, showing orientation of houses with service areas facing motor way and living areas facing parkland.

that the alternative to capital investment in better housing was "state intervention, with all the evils attendant upon that type of paternalism." That his brand of capitalism, which asked tenants to "give up many of the uncouth liberties they enjoyed in their old environments and substitute a reign of order and convention for what had been social anarchy,"[28] might be equally paternalistic apparently did not occur to Lewis. He categorically rejected the role of government and philanthropy in assuming responsibility for sheltering America's less privileged classes because, in his mind, this would have amounted to a suppression of democracy. Lewis argued that private developers, not public agencies or even philanthropic organizations, must be educated about and convinced of the economic and social advantages of developing affordable housing. By economically meeting the vast demand for low-cost homes, Lewis believed, private builders could reap their greatest profits, and in the process transform the living conditions of an entire nation.[29]

The Buhl Foundation's board of managers endorsed Lewis's ambitious vision. Swayed by the economic and humanitarian arguments and the successful records of the case studies Lewis had examined, the board approved his request for $1,000 to study the potential for developing limited-dividend housing in Pittsburgh. Lewis used the money to hire Clarence Stein, Henry Wright, and Frederick Bigger.

Chatham Village evolved directly out of the site-specific studies done by Stein, Wright, and Bigger and bears many of the distinctive stamps of the community planning ideals of the RPAA. Though they were neither the project's architects nor its developers, Stein, Wright, and Bigger provided critical observations and advice that transformed Lewis's initial notions of housing development. While supporting his argument that a limited-dividend project represented a safe and socially responsible investment for the foundation, the consultants' recommendations almost wholly contradicted most of the other original premises of the project. Initially planned as a community of detached, low-income homes to be offered for sale, Chatham Village materialized as rental row housing for the middle class. The modified development was successful from the beginning, and its developers and designers were proud to hold it up as a model of limited-dividend housing.

The Buhl Foundation provided the consultants with the following directives:

1. That it would be inadvisable to proceed with the work unless it were possible to make it a fairly large building operation, that is to say, one of 100 or 150 houses at least.
2. That the sale rather than rental of the houses is preferred by the Foundation.
3. That for sale purposes in Pittsburgh, free-standing houses are essential.
4. That the selling price must be kept as low as possible.[30]

Of these givens, only the first steered the project throughout its development. The main idea behind a large-scale project was that it could make use of economies of scale, including efficient site planning and construction savings through standardization of house plans, division of labor, and discount material purchasing. Such consolidation of effort would allow the foundation to provide more homes and amenities at less cost than the ordinary speculative builder. Chatham Village was constructed true to these precepts. Its first phase yielded 129 housing units, and the second phase increased the number to 197. Henry Wright expressed satisfaction with the economy of Chatham Village's construction in 1935, writing, "The project suggests that 125 [sic] dwellings, the number completed in the first section, are enough to secure decided advantages through large-scale operations."[31]

The three remaining premises fell under the scrutiny of the consultants. Based on his own observations of the market, Lewis had assumed that freestanding, single-family homes were the only type of housing that would sell in Pittsburgh. When his experts informed him that he could not

Figure 2.14. Chatham Village under construction, 1931

both serve his target market and make a profit by building this type of home, Lewis revised his plans. His other assumptions, all predicated upon this one, collapsed without it.

Certain constraints governed the location for Chatham Village as well as the development process. The Buhl Foundation assumed that residents would work in Pittsburgh's downtown business district, so the community needed to be close by for commuting convenience, and the land would have to be available at a price that allowed a safe investment return. Three tracts were seriously considered; all remained undeveloped and reasonably priced due to their steep topography. The most promising of these was the forty-five-acre former Bigham estate in the Mt. Washington area of the Nineteenth

Ward, a rugged plateau 1,220 feet above sea level and a formidable 500 vertical feet above the junction of the Allegheny, Monongahela, and Ohio Rivers.

Long known as Coal Hill, the high plateau was extensively mined from Revolutionary times through the 1800s. In 1851, Coal Hill's name was changed to Mt. Washington in honor of the young general who, from this vantage point, had once made a survey of the confluence of the Allegheny and Monongahela Rivers and seen the strategic position of Pittsburgh would hold as "Gateway to the West." While the Golden Triangle below became the city's bustling business center, Mt. Washington remained farmland for the few who had settled there, including Thomas Bigham.[32]

After the construction of the Monongahela Incline in 1870 made transportation to the peak of Mt. Washington available, the hilltop began to flourish as a bedroom community to downtown. Surveyors laid out a grid of streets over the steep sides of the hill, using Shiloh Street as the main corridor, and speculative developers filled in the building lots with modest single-family homes.[33] The Bigham property retained a rural character into the 1930s, however, largely as a result of a topography so steep that denser development was not thought to be feasible.

To the Buhl Foundation and its consultants, the advantages of this site included a size large enough for an experiment in neighborhood planning and a location that was close to downtown but adjacent to an existing city park and in a relatively unpolluted area. The importance of the latter cannot be overstated. Ralph E. Griswold, Chatham Village's landscape architect, provided a vivid picture of Pittsburgh's polluted atmosphere during its industrial years: "Abandoned to uncontrolled exploitation by commerce and industry the entire landscape—sky, trees, buildings, and rivers—was befouled by the black bituminous smoke. Even the bees made bituminous honey. Pittsburghers' lungs were gray. Streams became sewers."[34] In the context of the general degradation of Pittsburgh's environment, the relatively bucolic nature of the Big-ham estate made it especially attractive for a garden city–inspired project. Last but not least, a socioeconomic study commissioned by the Buhl Foundation (discussed further in chapter 4) revealed the Bigham estate to be surrounded by a "substantial, conservative, middle-class community."[35] This was, of course, a most desirable characteristic for ensuring the new development's stability.

A site-planning study conducted by Frederick Bigger in October 1930 clinched the decision to purchase the Bigham property. Bigger found, "Hillside land in the Pittsburgh dis-trict is poorly and wastefully developed. . . . Such land is usu-ally regarded as 'cheap.' It could prove a profitable investment, however, to the developer who budgeted judiciously for grad-ing, utilities, and the amenities that would make the develop-ment attractive to would-be residents."[36] A caveat, however, was declared by Bigger and by Stein and Wright, who had conducted a feasibility study of the Bigham tract: freestand-ing houses would be out of the question. Bigger wrote, "The cost of building houses on this tract, after it is graded, cannot differ materially from the cost of building similar houses on prepared tracts in other parts of the city. The controlling fac-tor is the 'site cost.'" His study described a development in which houses were grouped compactly, permitting "a stan-dardization which is highly desirable," around an undivided garden plot that would be held in common.[37] Bigger also em-phasized the importance of quality construction and ameni-ties in securing the value of the proposed development against the cost of the land, grading, and other improve-ments. To illustrate his ideas, Bigger enclosed sketches that, while more rigid and less imaginative than Stein and Wright's plans, bear a distinct similarity to Chatham Village as it was eventually built.

In their report of December 29, 1930, Stein and Wright reported findings similar to Bigger's. Lewis had hoped to offer houses priced in the $6,500 to $9,000 price range to clerical and skilled manual workers earning between $2,000 and $2,500 a year. But Stein and Wright noted in the beginning of their report:

We find that within the Pittsburgh district building costs will be at least as high as those at Radburn. Cost of roads, grading, and yard work per unit of free-standing houses will be greater. The overhead expenses of the Foundation should be as much if not more than those of the City Housing Corporation, which has had much longer experience. Therefore unless the Foundation is willing to accept a smaller return, it will be necessary to sell similar houses at a higher price than at Radburn. It is our present belief that the selling price of such houses would be between $9,500 and $12,000.[38]

Stein and Wright asserted that row housing would be a more economical alternative. From an architectural point of view, they added, "we would prefer to see the whole property developed in this way, for it would give not only more and cheaper houses but better looking houses and would permit the grouping of garages."[39] Stein and Wright were not adamant about this point, concentrating their analysis on detached housing as Lewis had requested. They nevertheless made their opinions clear by submitting an alternative study, which demonstrated that the Bigham site would accommodate 128 row houses built to sell for between $7,860 and $9,042 each, or only 80 detached houses priced at a prohibitive $10,500 each.[40]

The recommendations submitted by Bigger, Stein, and Wright led Charles Lewis to reconsider his commitment to building single-family homes. The fact that, as he had already observed in his initial report to the managers, "all types of housing have been built successfully under the limited-dividend plan"[41] may have made him more open to persuasion. In the final report they wrote to the board, authorized by Lewis and submitted in April 1931, Stein and Wright dealt solely with the row housing option.

The decision to give up detached, single-family houses called into question the assumptions that residents would have low incomes and that they would buy their homes.

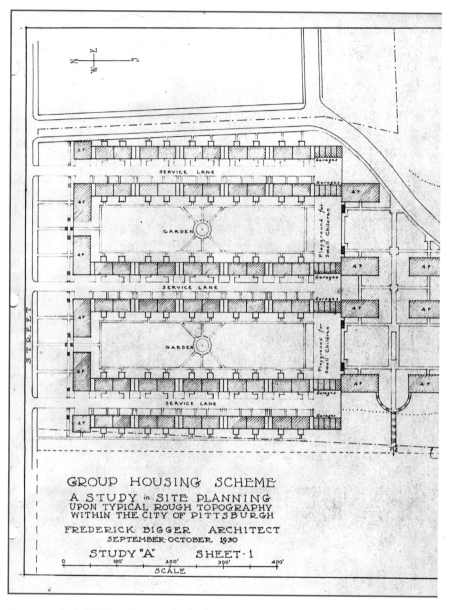

Figure 2.15. Frederick Bigger's site study plan for the Bigham property development, 1930

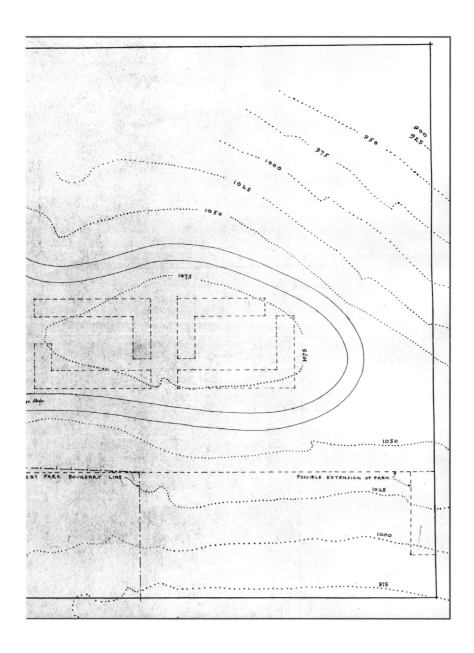

950

900
925

975

1000

1025

1050

1075

1075

1050

ENT PARK BOUNDARY LINE

POSSIBLE EXTENSION OF PARK

1025

1000

975

59

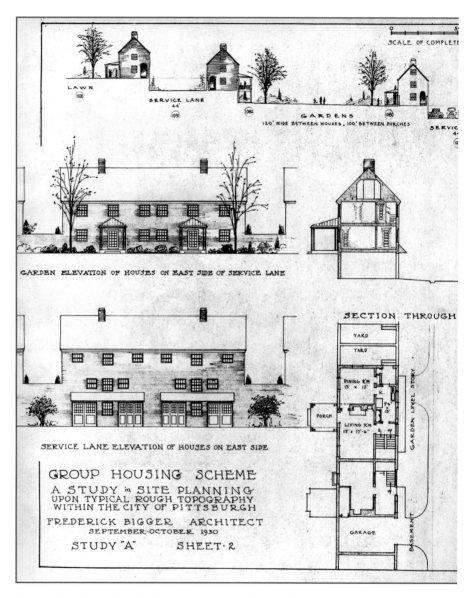

Figure 2.16. Frederick Bigger's plans of sections and elevations for the Bigham property development, 1930

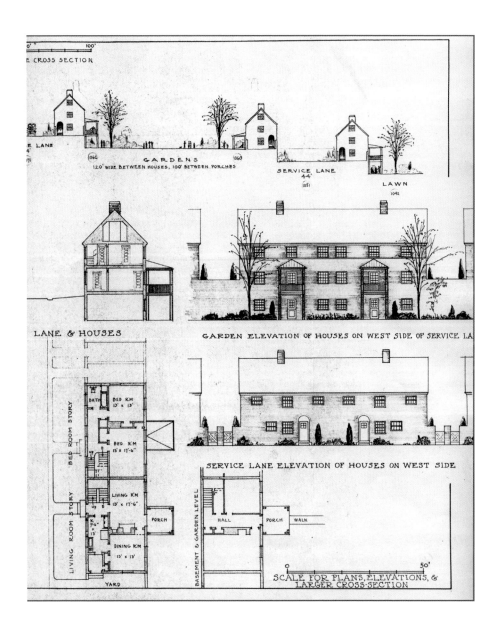

CROSS SECTION

LANE

GARDENS
120' WIDE BETWEEN HOUSES, 100' BETWEEN PORCHES

SERVICE LANE
44'
1051

LAWN
1042

1062 1060

LANE & HOUSES

GARDEN ELEVATION OF HOUSES ON WEST SIDE OF SERVICE LA.

BATH

BED RM
13' x 13'

BED RM
13' x 17'-6"

LIVING RM
13' x 17'-6"

PORCH

DINING RM
13' x 13'

BED ROOM STORY

LIVING ROOM STORY

YARD

SERVICE LANE ELEVATION OF HOUSES ON WEST SIDE

HALL

PORCH

WALK

BASEMENT & GARDEN LEVEL

SCALE FOR PLANS, ELEVATIONS, &
LARGER CROSS-SECTION

0 50'

61

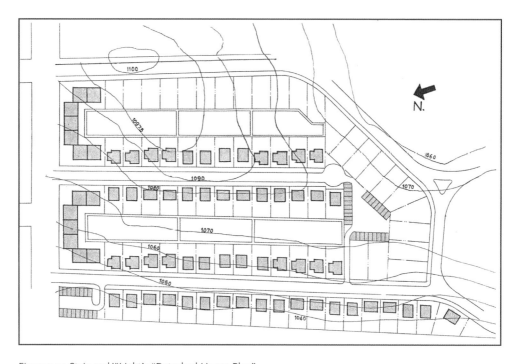

Figure 2.17. Stein and Wright's "Detached House Plan"

Though Stein and Wright stopped short of recommending that the Buhl Foundation revise its target market, Bigger did not. In the conclusion of his report to the Buhl Foundation, Bigger broached the risk of trying to provide housing for people of low income during hard economic times and noted, "there is a higher income group which is nevertheless on the border line between the [low-income] group and those whose housing offers no problem." Evicted from their homes during the worsening Depression, people of moderate means faced a shortage of decent, affordable housing. Bigger advised Lewis to protect his investment by aiming, first, to demonstrate successfully the practicality of limited-dividend development to the middle class and only later, when economic conditions were more stable, to build for low-income families.[42]

Herbert Emmerich, vice president of the City Housing

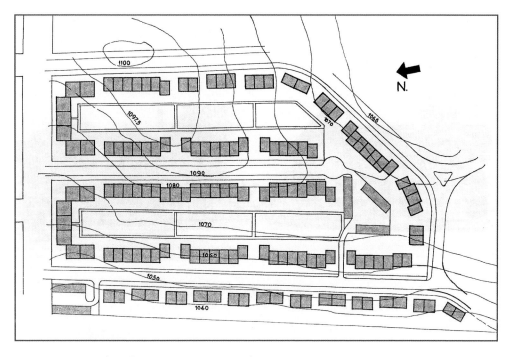

Figure 2.18. Stein and Wright's "Interior Row House Plan"

Corporation, corroborated Bigger's opinion. In November 1930, Emmerich accepted Lewis's invitation to visit Pittsburgh and make firsthand observations on the housing situation in general and the Buhl Foundation's proposed project in particular. Emmerich surmised that families earning between $2,500 and $3,600 a year, slightly more than Lewis's original intended market, could afford to buy homes that cost $8,000 to $12,000, of which there were few in the extant housing market. He went on to say that this income group would be the best target for the Buhl Foundation project because, being composed of white-collar workers and junior executives, it was very stable.[43] Emmerich also believed, based on his experience at Radburn, that members of the higher income bracket would better appreciate the amenities of a well-planned community.

Lewis was disappointed, but, trusting in his experts' unanimous advice, he conceded to raise the income level of his target market. A project for the middle class would be better than no project at all; he rationalized that once the foundation's limited-dividend project proved profitable, private capital would invest in other, similar schemes. Additionally, Lewis came to believe that as more of the middle class moved into this new housing, low-income groups would benefit by moving into the better dwellings that the middle class had vacated.[44]

Ultimately, the decision to build for the middle class and to abandon the plan for single-family homes put an end to the notion that the homes would be built for sale. Although families with higher incomes were more likely to be able to afford down payments, they were considered less likely to be interested in purchasing anything but detached houses. Indeed, Herbert Emmerich declared in his report to the Buhl Foundation, "The houses for sale in Pittsburgh should be free-standing, even if only a narrow side yard is maintained. The prejudice against buying attached houses is so great that it is deemed unwise to experiment in this respect."[45] Lewis also expressed concern, noting that single-family houses built in rows, separated by party walls, had never been sold in Pittsburgh.[46]

The project concept thus changed from that of a long-term housing solution for low-income families to a short-term solution for the middle class. Modern row houses, available at moderate rents, were to provide a middle-class alternative to high-rent apartments in run-down slums for those unable to take out a mortgage. In hindsight, Henry Wright summed up the overall change in the project concept by saying, "Though it was improbable that the Pittsburgh home-seeker would accept houses in groups for purchase, yet it was thought better to build something clearly within the price range of those needing the houses, and if necessary to rent instead of attempting to sell."[47]

In June 1931, when ground was broken for Chatham Village, Lewis delivered the five objectives that would guide the development of the new community:

1. To demonstrate the social and economic advantages of the large-scale garden homes community.
2. To demonstrate the advantages of social and economic security that are to be had from rental rather than purchase in a community managed from a long-term investment viewpoint.
3. To demonstrate that it is possible to build and operate such a community so as to yield a moderate but satisfactory investment return. The project is in no sense philanthropic. It is designed to be commercially practicable.
4. To develop new ideas and higher standards in house design and large-scale community planning.
5. Particularly to develop an appreciation of the contributions which may be made by competent site planning to large-scale hillside developments.[48]

More broadly stated than the four assumptions that guided the initial studies of Stein and Wright, this list embraced the shift from for-sale to rental structures, hinted at the unconventional housing type to be marketed, and glossed over the change in the income group to be served. It was this list of objectives that ultimately came to serve as a benchmark of Chatham Village's success. So great was Lewis's commitment to what he had built that he seemed to have forgotten what he had planned: a development to solve the housing crisis of lower-income families. If abandoning his ideal of providing the opportunity for home ownership to the lower class had been a disappointing setback for Lewis, his writing did not betray this. He proved his new devotion to his middle-income market with a flurry of articles in which he championed the housing needs of the "forgotten middle class."[49] In November 1931, his report to the board of managers, entitled "Housing: A Program for Administration," shows the zeal that attended his conversion:

In setting up a project on a rental, instead of a sale basis, the Foundation has paved the way for a demonstration in management quite as unique and useful as the demonstration in community planning and house design. No feature of the Foundation's plan has attracted more general attention and approval than the commitment to rental operation of these properties with long term view. The foreclosure tragedies of recent months in hundreds and thousands of American families have painfully demonstrated the fallacy of our previous emphasis on the desirability of home ownership for families of marginal income. It has been abundantly demonstrated that our economic and financial systems are not yet organized to give any guarantee of economic security to the average family that embarks upon the doubtful experiment of home ownership. It is clearly apparent that under proper management a far greater degree of social, as well as economic, security can be had through tenancy than through home ownership.[50]

Lewis also had the opportunity to share his newfound ardor for rental properties on a national level. The widely circulated plans for the Buhl Foundation's million-dollar-housing project earned him an invitation in June 1931 to serve on the Committee on Large Scale Operations of the President's Conference on Home Building and Home Ownership. Organized by President Herbert Hoover to address concerns over the increasing number of mortgage foreclosures, the conference considered ways to improve housing conditions, develop a sound and lasting system for home financing, and bring stability to real estate values. It was attended by thousands of participants from public agencies and private industry, including the nation's foremost experts on real estate, home financing, neighborhood planning, zoning, residential architecture and construction, domestic science, and methods of prefabrication.[51]

The conference's very name suggested its bias in favor of home ownership for American families. In spite of this, Lewis was able to convince his committee's chairman, Alfred K. Stern, director of the Julius Rosenwald Fund, a housing development company that had demonstrated the feasibility of low-income rental apartments in Chicago, that home ownership was not the answer to the nation's housing crisis. Lewis provided Stern with a copy of a study done as part of the Buhl Foundation's development research entitled "Housing Problems for Salaried Workers." Conducted by the University of Pittsburgh's Bureau of Business Research, the report proved that home owners in Pittsburgh paid more for their dwellings than renters did. Stern liked the study so much that he incorporated it into his committee's final report to the conference and used Lewis's ideas as ammunition to attack President Hoover's insistence on home ownership. Calling for tax exemptions for limited-dividend companies to aid private builders in constructing urban apartment communities, Stern advocated the creation of one large, national, limited-dividend corporation composed of privately owned smaller corporations and supervised by a national housing authority. The next year, Congress approved federal loans for limited-dividend companies in the Emergency Relief and Construction Act. Two year later, Congress boosted its support of limited-dividend corporations by authorizing insured mortgages for them.[52]

Clarence Stein, writing about Chatham Village in *Toward New Towns for America*, indulged in his own rant against home ownership, holding up the rental policy at Chatham Village as a model of sound economic and social planning. He compared the positive Chatham Village experience, in which the Buhl Foundation received an average 4.2 percent annual net return on its investment with the full investment paid off out of earnings in thirty years, to the negative experience at Sunnyside, where housing units were sold. There, he writes, residents found that "owning [their] own home was merely another form of tenancy" when hard times hit and they could no longer pay the interest on their mortgages. Though the residents "owned" their homes, the lending institutions actually controlled them, and exercised their right of foreclosure when residents lost their jobs, incomes, and savings during the Depression. Ultimately, many residents lost their homes at Sunnyside, and the City Housing Corporation, which had developed them, was attacked by the angry residents and went bankrupt. The comparison between Chatham Village and Sunnyside, Stein writes, demonstrated "the fallacy of the American faith, almost a religious belief, in 'home owner-ship.'"[53]

Henry Wright similarly named the rental policy at Chatham Village as one of "two very important things" demonstrated by the project. Wright made the argument from the developer's point of view, noting, "there is no very great gap between renting and selling. In selling houses on long terms, the Foundation would not be relieved of responsibility anyway for a long period of years. It might quite as well assume the responsibilities of ownership and management."[54] Wright concurred with Stein's opinion that the residents would be happier with rental contracts than with mortgages, since "a house seldom serves the family for the mortgage period," and rental contracts were more easily shed than ownership obligations when a family wanted to move on.[55]

Stein and Wright also both believed that Chatham Village demonstrated the advantage of well-designed grouped housing over conventional, single-family, detached units for the young, middle-class market. Chatham Village had consistently high occupancy rates, long waiting lists, and low tenant turnover. Stein and Wright held that this popularity, in turn, demonstrated that a housing type's suitability to its target population, not its conformity to traditional market standards, should guide decisions about its design. Henry Wright, always a strong proponent of grouped housing, took this idea one step further, arguing that row houses filled a significant gap in the existing market. He wrote: "In fact, the Chatham Village experiment [demonstrates] that our young people of the more well-to-do classes are not satisfied with their present housing accommodations. Their available choice now is between an expensive single house and a small residential-type apartment. It is very certain that no amount of abstract argument could have convinced such young people that they should live in a 'row house'; but when superior row houses were built at Chatham, they attracted young people who migrated from their natural locations in Pittsburgh's east end."[56]

Ultimately, Chatham Village's departures from its original premises were the very points on which it was most influential. Stein, Wright, and Bigger brought a revolutionary set of ideas about urban density, open space, hillside site planning, and residential community design to Lewis's initial plan. These initiatives transformed Chatham Village from an ordinary tract of single-family houses for sale into a far more compelling demonstration.

three   Design for a Modern Village

 The Buhl Foundation broke ground for the first phase of Chatham Village in spring 1931, and the first 129 houses were completed the next year. Great publicity surrounded the community during construction, and on Chatham Village's opening day, twenty thousand people waited in line to see the houses in their as-yet unlandscaped grounds. The project enjoyed an occupancy rate of above 99 percent in its first year and immediately returned a profit to the Buhl Foundation. Charles Lewis confidently attributed the devel-

Figure 3.1. Chatham Village Christmas celebration, 1930s

opment's success to the thoroughness of economic, site planning, sociological, and architectural studies performed over
the course of two years, but these were not the only factors.

By timing the construction to occur when building activity—and therefore prices—reached a low ebb, the planners of
Chatham Village amplified the project's cost efficiency. Moreover, Lewis applied modern ideas about economies of scale
and mass production borrowed from the revolutionary success of the automobile industry. At Chatham Village, clustering of buildings, standardization of design, shared party walls,
foundations that doubled as retaining walls, and discount

bulk purchase of materials all demonstrated the success of large-scale construction methods. Planners even determined the height of the houses using modern laws of technological efficiency; they found that they could erect a maximum of two stories without employing expensive towers or hoisting equipment.[1] Charles Lewis and Henry Wright shared a belief that the solution to the national housing problem depended upon the revolution of the building industry into vertically organized, mass production units and building entire neighborhoods rather than scattered dwellings. Such a transformation would put good housing, like automobiles, within the reach of multitudes.[2]

Paradoxically, even as they exploited modern technology to build Chatham Village, the project's planners wove a self-conscious, nostalgic regard for the past into the look, feel, and even sound of the new community. The Buhl Foundation chose a name for the neighborhood—out of a brainstorm of words including Washington, Colonial, Hill, Treemont, and Green—that incorporated historical associations with the beginnings of Pittsburgh (William Pitt was also known as the Earl of Chatham). In an urban neighborhood, the name Chatham Village also connoted the picturesque colonial past represented by the image of a New England village green.[3] The foundation chose street names that also have historical associations: Bigham Road, obviously, with the Bigham estate; Olympia with the adjacent city park; Pennridge Road with name of William Penn, who once owned the Chatham Village property; and Sulgrave Road with the ancestral home of George Washington in England.

Architects Ingham and Boyd designed the homes to be elegantly understated yet judiciously detailed in the vocabulary of the then-popular Colonial Revival and Arts and Crafts styles. Their choices of traditional building materials and details reflected a contemporary trend toward idealization of the preindustrial past, epitomized by the reconstruction of Colonial Williamsburg, which had been ongoing since 1926 and

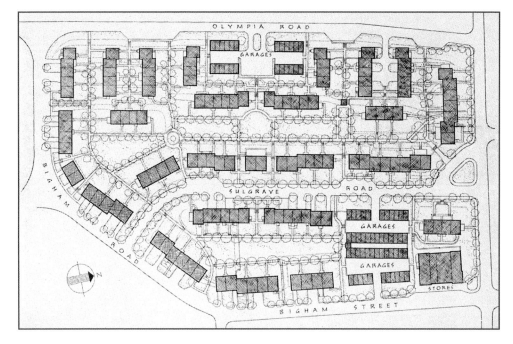

Figure 3.2. Stein and Wright's plan of the first unit of Chatham Village

strongly influenced popular taste in everything from architecture to reading material. While construction methods at Chatham Village looked forward, the community's aesthetic was focused resolutely on the past.[4]

The first phase of Chatham Village, an eight-and-a-half-acre superblock, was modified from a similar superblock pioneered at Radburn. Bounded by Virginia Avenue (an existing street through the Mt. Washington neighborhood) to the north and private perimeter roadways surrounding it on the other three sides, the first phase constitutes a rectangle with the southern corner clipped off at a slant. On the west side, the development is adjacent to Olympia Park, a municipal green space that extends the Village's twenty-nine-acre greenbelt. Planners developed this greenbelt, which was composed

Figure 3.3. The most formal of Chatham Village's courtyards

of land too steep or otherwise unusable for housing, with trails and plantings according to a specially prepared "Woodland Development" design. Connected groups of two to seven houses face inward around three main interior courtyards of different shapes and sizes: one is a triangle, another a trapezoid, and a third is a long, formal rectangle, emphasized by a soldier-straight allée of trees.

Henry Wright, who largely developed the site plan, proceeded by using the topography as a determining influence.[5] The row houses are stepped down a series of wide terraces, and their foundations serve as retaining walls. Though all of the houses are two stories, those located higher on the terraces have unobstructed second-floor views over the rooftops of those lower down, thus gracefully solving one of the most commonly cited problems—dim interiors—of row house living. The site's steep contours also allow for basements that are half above ground and thus well lit.

The homes include service entrances that face the street or cul-de-sac, but the front doors open onto communally held lawns, gardens, and what were, in the 1930s, children's play areas complete with sandboxes. Seven pavilions and toolsheds, treated as garden follies, have seven different designs. Instead of continuous sidewalks, pedestrian walks within the central grounds provide connections between the house units. Careful efforts at grading eliminated strenuous climbs, while some stone garden steps on the interior walks add visual interest.

In 1931, a social study of the Bigham property's neighbors had revealed that, surprisingly, over one-third of them commuted to work by car. Stein and Wright's solution to the inevitable presence of automobiles at Chatham Village was modified from their approach at Radburn. Stein believed that the urban grid may have functioned for the nineteenth-century walking city, but that the introduction of the automobile made it deadly to pedestrians. In observing places where old

Figure 3.4. Perspective drawing of the first unit

Figure 3.5. Terracing of the row houses on the site's steep hills

walking cities and towns had adapted themselves to the automobile, he rued the fact that "the roadbed was the children's
main play space," while "parked cars, hard gray roads and garages replaced gardens."[6] At Chatham Village, as at Radburn,
Stein and Wright strove to create a living environment that
was served, but not dominated, by cars. The planners provided for access to the community via a loop of peripheral
roads off of Virginia Avenue. Thirty-two of the first-phase
houses, which back directly onto the peripheral roads, have
integral garages on the basement level, recessed so as not to
be noticeable except when viewed head-on. The rest of the
units, located in the interior of the block, make use of three

Figure 3.6. Pedestrian paths on an interior courtyard lead to sandboxes and one of Chatham Village's quaintly designed toolsheds.

walled, communal garage compounds. There is one Radburn-style cul-de-sac. A small shopping center of four units is located at the corner of the development nearest to downtown Pittsburgh. Its original tenants were a drug store, grocery store, beauty shop, and Boggs and Buhl department store outlet, which, together, served the residents' immediate needs.

Figure 3.7. Garden steps conquer steep topography and add visual interest.

First-phase houses—available in one-, two-, and three-bedroom models—are all single-family units with private entrances. Stein and Wright's experience with two-family houses at Sunnyside had taught them that these units were more likely to have vacancies, for the lower apartments tended to be noisy while the upper ones were too far removed

Figure 3.8. Homes in which rear walls face peripheral roads have recessed integral garages.

Figure 3.9. One of the three garage compounds that provide parking for units without integral garages

Figure 3.10. A "shopping corner" designed in scale and harmony with Chatham Village residences, c. 1950s

from the gardens.[7] Due to sharp variations in elevation, most Chatham Village houses have two ground-floor levels, leading to some variations of the floor plan that would not have been necessary at a level site.[8] Each house consists of a full basement (containing laundry and garage or, where basement windows face west, a sunroom), a first floor with living room, dining room or dinette, and kitchen or kitchenette, and a second floor with bedrooms and bath.

The ideal of the practical modern American home governed the architectural design at Chatham Village. When it opened, each unit boasted a laundry and such up-to-date kitchen amenities as steel cabinets, electric refrigeration, overheat regulation, forced draft ventilators, automatically controlled natural-gas-burning furnaces, and hot water heat-

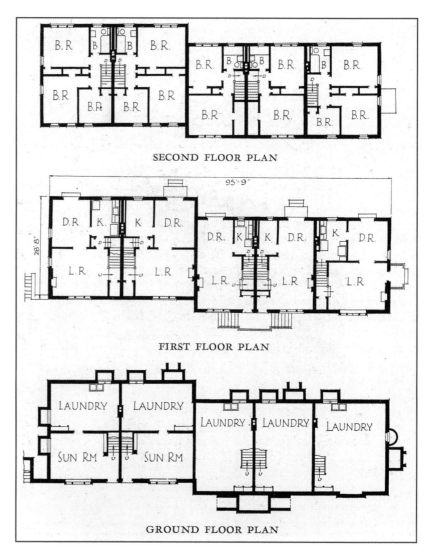

Figure 3.11. Typical floor plan of a five-unit row containing two- and three-bedroom units

Figure 3.12. An original kitchenette furnished by Boggs and Buhl department store for a model home in Chatham Village's second phase, 1936

ers. Living and bedrooms were not large but were light, airy, and simply and elegantly finished with hardwood floors, Georgian-style moldings, and white plaster walls. The Buhl Foundation's budget allowed for redecorating every five years.

The buildings' architect, William Boyd, explained that practical concerns, not adherence to the strict conventions of any architectural style or period, governed the design of the Chatham Village homes. He wrote: "The plan of the houses is American. It is fundamentally the old reception hall type omitting the wall between the hall and the living room. For years this type of plan has been studied and developed because, for the small house, it has proven to give the maximum of usable floor space. . . . Even if the house is an interior one, having no side windows, ample light and ventilation may be obtained."[9]

Although he worked within a consistent design vocabulary that may be seen as Georgian Revival pared down to its

Figure 3.13. Living room in a Chatham Village home

essentials, Boyd resisted attempts to label his style at Chatham Village. He maintained that it was "rational modern American architecture;"[10] neither period revival nor modern in the European sense, but an elegant, New World solution to practical concerns. Although Boyd wrote that he had endeavored to avoid "unnecessary gables" or other architectural features applied solely for ornament's sake, his partner, Charles Ingham, explained why Chatham Village was not modern architecture. In Germany, where the Bauhaus began, minimalism in building design had become an economic necessity. In making a virtue of this necessity, Ingham explained, the Germans had rationalized that their simplified designs were expressive of the machine age, and architects in other coun-

Figure 3.14. Bedroom in a demonstration home in Chatham Village's second unit, 1936

tries had embraced this rationale. Yet the Modernist fashion was bound to be temporary, for it went against human nature to resist symbolic adornment, to be satisfied with mere utilitarian protection from the elements. Ingham wrote, "The architects of Chatham Village have recognized the value of simplicity in design but have endeavored to avoid overstressing it. . . . There was no impulse to express the machine age in its design, but rather to create a retreat from the machine age" in architecture neither overtly Modernistic nor traditional.[11]

In consultation with the Buhl Foundation, Ingham and Boyd chose exterior materials with long-term maintenance costs rather than short-term construction expenses in mind, intending the red-brick walls and Peach Bottom slate roofs to last "indefinitely" and the limestone doorways and iron porches to weather more slowly than wood.[12] The houses display small variations in exterior detail, which, while understated, forestall monotony in their appearance. Both hipped and gabled roofs appear, and quoins, cornices, and treatments of the large living room windows all differ subtly from house to house. Stone cartouches over some doorways and on some end walls represent the coats of arms of three statesmen who, at various times, controlled the land upon which Chatham Village was built: William Pitt, Earl of Chatham; the Marquis Duquesne; and George Washington. Aside from this, extraneous ornament is kept to a minimum, and the development's architectural richness relies upon the effects created by the massing, terracing, and rhythmic staggering of the row houses themselves.

Planners anticipated a second phase of Chatham Village from the beginning, but left the timing to be decided. In 1934, the board of managers of the Buhl Foundation authorized the preparation of site plans, but due to high costs, did not under-

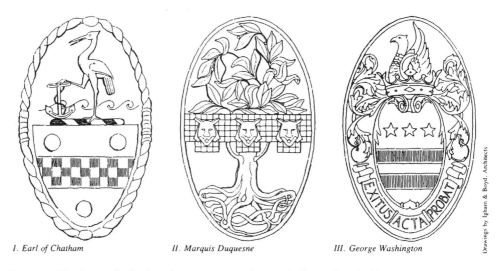

I. Earl of Chatham   *II. Marquis Duquesne*   *III. George Washington*

Drawings by Igham & Boyd. Architects.

Figure 3.15. The designs for the three decorative cartouches on Chatham Village buildings

Figure 3.16. George Washington cartouche above doorways

take a construction program in that year. In 1935, however, prices came down, and Lewis and the managers were anxious to underscore the lessons of large-scale limited-dividend development. Lewis suggested to the board six reasons to consider moving ahead with the second phase at this time.

First, the success of the first phase occurred in the face of unparalleled adverse economic conditions. Tenancy reached 100 percent in 1935, and the turnover rate, caused chiefly by business transfers, remained low, presenting few opportunities for those on the waiting list to move in. The net return to the foundation was healthy, which produced payments into amortization and maintenance reserves as expected. Lewis believed that the economy was about to turn a corner, that rents in Pittsburgh were certain to rise, and that the time was thus ripe to prepare more units for the market.[13]

Moreover, demand for homes was increasing. Lewis noted that Chatham Village was unable to accommodate all the families who currently wanted to live there. In addition, it occasionally lost good tenants who had outgrown the existing houses. He suggested that a second phase, containing a number of four-bedroom units with an extra bath, would make the community more flexible for more kinds of families.

Due to the nearly complete suspension of residential building in Allegheny County during the previous five years, a huge potential housing shortage had occurred. The need was exacerbated because the county's population had grown by 16 percent since the foundation had done its preliminary studies, and the number of families had grown by 23 percent. It was assumed that, when the economy recovered, significant demands for new homes would be created by marriages and families deferred during the Depression, and the expected economic upswing would allow a large number of young couples and families to escape their current doubled-up conditions. Thus, smaller houses and apartments would be in demand because modern families were of smaller size.

Lewis also maintained that the addition of 68 new homes

to Chatham Village would strengthen the investment by creating a more efficient management unit and a more stable community. Economies of scale would save the foundation money. Lewis reasoned that 197 homes could be operated with virtually the same management staff as was required for 129, and the increase in families would enhance the rental value of the commercial corner, making it possible to find business tenants for the then-vacant storefront. More importantly, Chatham Village needed to be big enough to survive independent of the fortunes of the neighborhood around it. Lewis regarded the first phase as "the smallest possible demonstration of a large-scale operation."[14] With close to 200 homes, he believed, its security would be assured.

The foundation could obtain favorable bids almost immediately. Though construction costs were approximately 10 percent higher in 1935 than in 1932, this excess cost distributed over the entire property represented an increase of approximately 3 percent, which would be absorbed by management economies and increased commercial rentals without raising house rents above the present schedules. Furthermore, the excess maintenance reserves would be left untouched.

Finally, the comparatively low bid prices would not last long. Lewis quoted "persons familiar with the construction industries" in claiming that "there is no reason for expectation of lower wage rates for the building trades in Pittsburgh in the next few years,"[15] and noted that, as the economy recovered, building costs were in fact likely to skyrocket as pent-up demand clamored for a short supply. The economic timing was right to build.

Lewis's instincts and research had led to a successful first phase at Chatham Village, and the board of managers did not doubt him now. They accepted the site plan for phase two, which had been prepared a year previously by Henry Wright in consultation with Ingham and Boyd and Ralph E. Griswold, the landscape architect for Chatham Village. Designed to integrate with phase one while providing variety in types

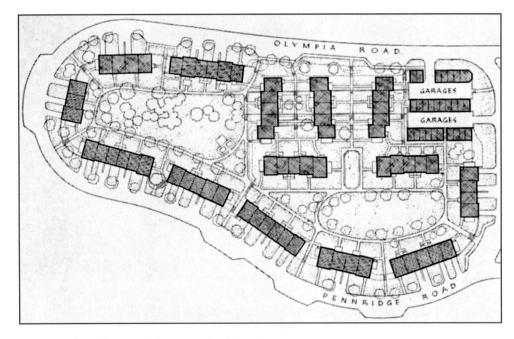

Figure 3.17. Plan of the second phase, completed in 1936

of gardens and houses,[16] phase two consisted of another single superblock, somewhat more curvilinear than the first, bounded by private perimeter roads and the Chatham Village greenbelt beyond. Built in 1935–1936, the new homes were set around two principal courtyards, one approximately trapezoidal, the other shaped like an archer's bow. Wright and his colleagues maintained the basic scheme of connected row houses. Units that backed to the road included basement garages; two more garage compounds were added to accommodate the vehicles of interior units.

The exterior design of the houses echoed that of phase one, with slight modifications: the limestone doorframes and cartouches were eliminated, and every house was given a covered front entrance. The architects also created seven four-bedroom, two-bath houses, which included dormers to accommodate the extra spaces. *Architectural Forum* raved about the harmonious design of phase two: "Proud of their handiwork should be the directors of the Village. For, when plans were organized for the 68-house unit recently completed, they made an exhaustive search for possible innovations, were forced to decide that the first job had been done well enough to serve as a model for subsequent units. True, another basic type was added to answer a demand for a larger house. . . . But by and large, the second unit is no more than an extension of the first."[17]

Like the first phase, the second phase quickly filled with tenants. In addition to extending and enlarging the community, the second phase of the project linked Chatham Village with the 1844 Greek revival manor house of the Bigham estate. Renamed Chatham Hall, the house served as a terminus of the development on the southern point of the hilltop and was remodeled for use as a venue for meetings, dramatics, hobby groups, and a village nursery school, which operated under the management of the residents until 1990, when it closed due to decreased enrollment.

Lewis liked to refer to Chatham Village as a garden community, and its landscape has always been one of its most attractive and distinguishing features. The clustering of the houses, relegation of automobile traffic to the perimeter, and near-complete elimination of private yards placed an emphasis on the community's abundant, park-like communal grounds as one of its primary attractions.[18] To enhance the appreciation of landscape and architecture alike, all unsightly utility and power lines at Chatham Village were buried underground, decades before this became common practice. Here, as in all of Stein and Wright's communities, landscape amenities were not a frivolous expense but a fundamental enhancement of community life.

Broadly speaking, there are really three landscapes at Chatham Village: the gardens around the houses, the recreational areas, and the "wilderness" greenbelt. Ralph E. Gris-

Figure 3.18. Chatham Village's grouped buildings and communal open spaces, 1936

wold, who also served as the landscape architect for Colonial Williamsburg,[19] created a landscape plan for the former Bigham estate that emphasized the architectural image of a village. Kentucky bluegrass lawns served as the background of the entire landscape picture, and Griswold emphasized the need for their maintenance. "If [the lawns] are well kept and vigorous they will be the community's greatest landscape asset," he wrote. "Comparatively few appreciate the difference between good and bad planting but all can judge the condition of a lawn."[20]

Against this grassy canvas, the trees stand out as the dis-

tinguishing feature of Chatham Village's landscape. Griswold integrated a stand of "Chatham oaks" from the Bigham estate into phase two of the housing development, and selected trees elsewhere for permanence and suitability to location. He noted, "This type of [comprehensive community] planning has the distinct advantage of controlling the selection and arrangement of its trees for community effect. This opportunity should be used to create a more rural atmosphere than is usual in city developments." He went on to say that "The village is distinguished primarily by its open areas and trees. By concentrating on trees and lawn less shrubbery will be necessary."[21]

Figure 3.19. Built in the second phase, seven four-bedroom, two-bath houses are recognizable by their third-story dormer windows.

Figure 3.20. Chatham Hall, a clubhouse and social center for residents of Chatham Village

Accordingly, the site plan and architecture of Chatham
Village minimized the need for much shrubbery. Careful consideration of grading in relation to walks and building lines
eliminated the need for screens. Since the architecture rested
"comfortably on the ground," there was no need for base
plantings, and Griswold observed, "the community grouping
eliminates the necessity of screening objectionable relations
of buildings."[22] Shrubbery was used only as ornament, border
planting, and covering of banks that were judged difficult to
keep in turf. Hedges, on the other hand, "provide protection
with the greatest economy of space," Griswold remarked.
"They maintain a dignified uniformity of foliage texture and
preserve a neat appearance. The inharmonious confusion of
planting on individual properties to suit a variety of tastes is
not unpleasant if unified by consistent hedging."[23] Since this

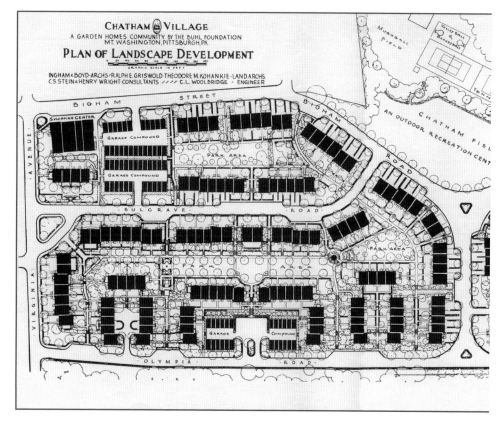

Figure 3.21. Landscape plan for Chatham Village

effect is best achieved by using the fewest possible varieties of hedge material, Griswold suggested only two, Barberry and Ibota Privet. He also recommended vines for certain walls, doorways, and openings, to contribute to the village atmosphere.

Griswold held adamant opinions on the boundary between individual expression through plantings and living amid a unified landscape. Since the Buhl Foundation wanted to encourage in tenants a sense of pride in their homes, and since the management could not possibly predict the individual needs and tastes of each family that might move in,

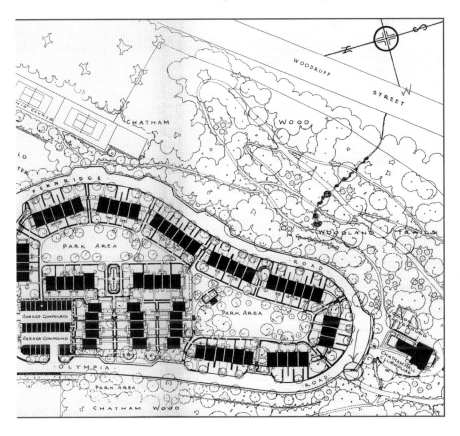

Griswold advocated that tenants be allowed as much latitude as possible in making landscape decisions in the immediate vicinities around the properties they occupied. He even went so far as to suggest that, although tenants would inevitably change, an interest in planting might be an added incentive to remain longer in Chatham Village and thus increase the development's long-term stability.

Griswold suggested that management make a gardening superintendent available to the initial tenants during construction, to offer advice about plantings and provide a justification for making a rigid restriction against employment of

Figure 3.22. Hedges divide private front gardens from public lawns.

commercial landscape gardeners or nurserymen to plant on individual properties. Such commercial gardeners were a menace to small property owners on Mt. Washington, Griswold said, and they had been the scourge of Sunnyside. By allowing individual planting through an official hired by the foundation, Griswold hoped to avoid similar consequences at Chatham Village.

Just to the east of the housing units, cupped by the joint of phase one and two, hilltop land was set aside for outdoor recreation areas: tennis, volleyball, and basketball courts; an open field for games; and community garden plots. In 1952, a rose garden was planted in memory of Mildred M. Lutz, a longtime Chatham Village resident and its first manager, at the crest of the hill, nearest the houses on Pennridge Road.

Fanning out from three sides of Chatham Hall to the valleys 250 feet below is Chatham Wood. This twenty-five-acre greenbelt, part of a woodland long known to Pittsburghers as Bigham's Woods, contains the last stand of the oaks that originally covered the Mt. Washington hilltop. The woodland plan that preserved these trees, prepared by landscape architect Theodore M. Kohankie, reflected the objectives of the Buhl Foundation, which appropriated $6,000 for the development of the woodlands: to open up the woods as completely as possible by building trails, while retaining its character as a woodland, not a park; and to concentrate new planting in strategic areas. By 1937, Chatham Village's landscape contained a total of 2,232 trees, shrubs, and vines, reflecting 68 different varieties, most of which were new to the land. The plan directed the planting of evergreen trees for the first time, for instance, as well as several varieties of native deciduous trees to provide touches of color and nuts and berries to attract wildlife. Tree labels were prepared and mounted. Two miles of trail were cleared and built, and along it two springs were turned into a waterfall and cascade which became centers for new planting. Below Chatham Hall, an area was cleared to serve as a picnic grove. Finally, the foundation installed a seven-foot fence, and reports indicated that vandalism subsequently ceased. The woodland plan was completed in stages over several years in the late 1930s and early 1940s.[24]

Chatham Village's greenbelt is viewed as one of its finest, most distinctive amenities. Today, when one enters Chatham Village from the busy city streets around it, one experiences a noticeable sense of having entered an urban oasis. Even the leafiest suburban enclave cannot compare with the green serenity of Chatham Village's park-like grounds, girded by a thick swath of wilderness.

This sense of isolation is no accident. Chatham Village

Figure 3.23. Fishing in Chatham Wood, c. 1940

was never supposed to form connections to the older community that surrounded it, except by roadway for automobile access. The planning principles behind the greenbelt were as much economic as environmental; they were designed to conserve the foundation's investment along with the trees. On this point, Lewis and Stein were both quite candid. "Chatham Village," Lewis wrote, "is extremely fortunate in having its own greenbelt around most of the property. This greenbelt provides for recreation and is a safeguard against possible undesirable environmental factors. Only for a distance of three blocks has Chatham been exposed to neighborhood changes."[25] As Stein noted, Chatham Village demonstrated that "a greenbelt, even one as small as that of Chatham, insu-

Figure 3.24. This photograph of walkers in Chatham Wood, the community's greenbelt, was featured on the cover of Clarence Stein's book, *Toward New Towns for America*.

lates a community from neighborhood depreciation and external annoyance."[26]

If the development of a greenbelt was one means of creating a buffer zone to isolate Chatham Village from changes in the surrounding community, another was Charles Lewis's "protective purchase" of neighboring properties. The Buhl Foundation acquired the first of these during construction of the first phase; over the next twenty years, the board of managers secured seven additional parcels of land, five of them strategically located at street intersections. The properties included a storeroom, which the foundation rented out, and seven residential buildings, two of which were demolished immediately upon purchase, and five of which were maintained "at considerable inconvenience" to the foundation during the years of the housing shortage.[27] In 1955, Lewis proposed to the managers that these remaining structures—located conspicuously at a corner where Chatham Village met the preexisting neighborhood—be razed at once, and that the cleared land be utilized for a final Chatham Village building campaign. He wrote:

Chatham Village should have a more dignified entrance than has been possible in the past. . . . Most persons who come to the Village, whether residents or visitors, approach it on Bigham Street and get their first impression at Virginia Avenue, where the orderly, attractive architecture of the Village is discredited by the tawdry appearance of the old buildings on the left. Over many years, it has been realized that it is desirable, by a modest additional building program, to "put a frame around the picture." It has been realized that such a program would enhance significantly the value of the present Village, not only from aesthetic standpoints but from sound investment considerations.[28]

Lewis identified four needs that had become apparent to him over twenty-three years of managing Chatham Village: additional garages, storage space, a gardeners' workshop, and one-bedroom apartments. Like the four-bedroom units added in phase two, the apartments were meant to expand housing options and make Chatham Village a more flexible, and therefore stable, community. Instead of moving away, families and individuals could simply move from one housing type to another as their needs changed. Lewis believed that apartments were necessary to serve three groups: young married couples without children, employed persons who found maintaining even a small house a chore, and elderly people who no longer needed all the rooms provided by larger homes and/or could no longer negotiate stairs.

Designed by Ingham, Boyd, and Pratt, the successor firm to Ingham and Boyd, and called Chatham Manor, the three-story building is constructed of brick on a steel frame in a simple, straightforward modern mode. Its materials, multi-

Chatham Village News

Vol. XXV   Pittsburgh, September 1, 1956   No. 1

Chatham Manor Previewed, Opened, Occupied

Figure 3.25. Chatham Manor apartment house, completed in 1956

paned window sash, and boxy massing make visual reference to the Chatham Village row houses across the road, but all ornament and details except for a cast stone cornice have been omitted. Inside, the building's nineteen apartments reflect a 1950s approach to "modern living." The dining nook, which Lewis noted had "proved unsatisfactory over many years" in the Chatham homes, was eliminated. Instead, living rooms were made large enough to accommodate dining as well as other family activities. All apartments were wired for television and air conditioning and included two telephone outlets. Bathrooms were fitted with rubber tile floors, ceramic tile walls, and fixtures Lewis called "high grade but not extravagant." "Streamlined" kitchens came equipped with ventilating fans, large storage closets, and package receivers. Bedrooms, Lewis reported proudly, "in every case accommodate twin beds."[29] Corridors were carpeted in the interest of "gracious and quiet living," and no two apartments were separated by as little as a single wall. "Noise interference from apartment to apartment has been virtually eliminated," boasted Lewis, in this "design for unexcelled privacy in apartment living."[30] An incinerator and rubbish room were on each floor, with laundry facilities, storage lockers for tenants, and the boiler room located in the basement. In contrast to most three-story apartment buildings, which functioned as walkups, Chatham Manor boasted an elevator. Lewis concluded a description of the building plans by claiming, "the apartment design and the provision of an elevator set a new and trailblazing standard for three-story apartment dwellings."[31]

With the completion of Chatham Manor, the full vision for Chatham Village was realized. Though the topography of the Bigham property was considered so rugged that development would be infeasible, the Buhl Foundation and its consultants proved this conventional wisdom wrong. The foundation bought the property at a discount and, through expert site planning that worked with, not against, the property's dramatic changes in grade, turned the site's drawbacks to advantages and substantially increased its value.

four The Social Life of a Planned Community

Just as the Buhl Foundation and its consultants planned the Chatham Village site to yield a societal and economic return, so too did they meticulously research and plan the social life of the neighborhood in order to bring about an ideal—and therefore a satisfied and profitable—community. Having created a demonstration in residential community design, the foundation maintained firm control over the community's management, maintenance, demographics, and social life to ensure the attractiveness of the buildings and grounds, the stability of the resident community, and, above all, the security of its own investment. The first step in planning the Village's social life took place even before the decision to build on the Bigham tract had been finalized. Prior to purchasing the property, the Buhl Foundation commissioned a sociological study of the area lying between it and Grandview Avenue, at the crest of the bluff of Mt. Washington.

The sociologist who conducted the study was Rose C. Weibel. In spring 1931, Weibel spent more than a week in the area, visiting more than fifty homes to learn about the social life and status of the neighborhood. She found that it was composed mainly of "well-behaved" Irish and German families whose wage-earning members worked as clerks, skilled tradesmen, and railroad men. Most commuted to jobs downtown by incline or automobile. Though there were large numbers of Catholics and Protestants in a fairly equal mix, it appeared that the neighborhood park, rather than any of the churches, served as the most active community center.

Weibel termed the Nineteenth Ward, in which the future Chatham Village was located, an "old" district, noting that its building stock consisted of mostly frame houses, though there were some newer properties clad in brick veneer. Some of Weibel's observations betrayed her personal judgment of the community's residents, as when she remarked, "These newer houses show the beginnings of some architectural appreciation in the neighborhood."[1] Although it was "not a reading community" (there were books in only two of the homes she visited), Weibel noted the tolerance of the residents, who showed "a tendency to assimilate new blood . . . and to get along with each other in spite of religious and racial differences." It was an established, stable neighborhood, in which home owners far outnumbered renters, and in which "with three exceptions those interviewed thought that the 'hill' was the finest place to live in the city, if not in the world. . . . And

Figure 4.1. Manor Street, Mt. Washington, 1931

there seems to be no exception at all to the rule that every family is living on the hill because a parent or relative had lived there before them. This makes for a certain stability and substantialness which is markedly characteristic of the hilltop population."[2] From Weibel's study, Charles Lewis concluded that the Bigham property possessed the qualities of simplicity, stability, and community loyalty that would make it an ideal context for his demonstration.[3]

As planned and constructed, however, Chatham Village has always been a community apart from the Mt. Washington neighborhood in which it was built. From the outset, the Buhl Foundation fostered separateness from the physical, economic, and social patterns of the larger area.[4] One early resident characterized the relationship between Chatham Village and Mt. Washington as "polite neighborliness," but other evidence suggests that the relationship may have been more mutually suspicious, if not overtly unfriendly, in tone. Chatham Village children, for instance, referred to their Mt. Washington classmates as "outsiders," and feared being stigmatized by them. Residents of Chatham Village and their Mt. Washington neighbors interacted at a few points of contact, such as the parent-teacher association and a local church, but "the social life of the Village [was], to a considerable degree, self-contained, as might have been predicted. Village residents, drawn from the same stratum of society, quickly formed new circles of friends in the Village itself."[5]

Physically, Chatham Village achieves its enclave effect through a cunning combination of topography and architectural design. As Weibel noted, the site, "has such sharply defined natural boundaries as to isolate it rather effectively from the surrounding hilltop sections. . . . [T]he section under consideration becomes a sort of knob, cut off" from the surrounding neighborhood on all sides."[6] Enclosed by a greenbelt on three sides, Chatham Village presents only one inhabited face to the neighborhood, and its expression is distinctly aloof. Rather than extend the existing grid, the planned community's private roads defy it as they embrace the superblock with their curvilinear forms. Chatham Village's "urban eden" of landscaped courtyards and gardens is not an amenity for the larger neighborhood, but clearly meant for residents alone; there is no formal gate or sign to welcome visitors. Houses literally turn their backs to the community at large, and the uniformity of Chatham Village's neo-Georgian brick row houses departs vividly from the surrounding neighborhood's preexisting variety of single-family homes.

Chatham Village's isolation from Mt. Washington is not as paradoxical as it may, at first, seem. The Buhl Foundation's housing project was a living laboratory for testing the planning ideals of Charles Lewis and the RPAA. The stability of

Figure 4.2. A circle of friends inside Chatham Village, 1932

the adjoining area was an important factor for the planned community's developers to consider, but only insofar as any economic decline or social unrest there was thought to constitute a threat to the serenity and security of Chatham Village. As a housing demonstration, it was a self-contained, singular enterprise; as a planned community, it was a premeditated ideal environment whose social life, like its physical form, required a degree of control. Chatham Village,

Figure 4.3. This aerial photograph of Chatham Village, taken in 1936, shows it in relation to the surrounding community.

therefore, has always had what amounts to its own form of local government. Its community administration has gone through two distinct phases: ownership and management by the Buhl Foundation from construction through 1959, followed by cooperative ownership by the residents from 1960 to the present.

Although it had been built by a philanthropy, one of the fundamental founding principles of Chatham Village was that it was emphatically *not* philanthropic housing. Residents and observers were to make no mistake: Chatham Village was a commercial, capitalist, for-profit venture. Charles Lewis believed that quality, affordable housing was the responsibility of private enterprise, not charity or the state, and that private enterprise had thus far shirked this duty due to a major flaw

in the building industry: it was controlled by greedy speculators who tried to excuse their failure to build modern,
planned, large-scale communities on the false basis that such
developments were financially unsound. Lewis sincerely believed that the success of Chatham Village would awaken the
social consciousness of American investors and ultimately
spark a national movement to provide housing for moderate-
to-middle income groups through the construction of comprehensively planned, limited-dividend projects.[7]

Lewis's insistence that his demonstration project earn a
profit meant that what looked like sympathetic social policy
at Chatham Village was often really driven by economic imperative. Certainly, social idealism was also a major driving
force behind the development of Chatham Village—the project was, after all, a didactic experiment in progressive community building. If it worked, it would demonstrate to an ill-
housed nation the advantages of large-scale, non-speculative,
socially and environmentally sensitive residential development. In the end, however, the success of the experiment depended upon a most unpredictable factor: the behavior of the
Village's tenants.

One way the Buhl Foundation sought to influence this
behavior was through design. Clarence Stein and Henry
Wright, America's foremost experts in designing physical
spaces to foster social goals, made decisions with the residents
in mind. From the choice to build in brick because "brick veneer seems to be the favorite" material among residents of
Mt. Washington[8] to the integration of different-sized units
throughout the Village, Stein and Wright aimed to assure tenant satisfaction and, therefore, investment security. The project's architecture and amenities encouraged tenant interaction as a way of fostering a community spirit that, it was
hoped, would make the Village a desirable place to live and
keep vacancies to a minimum. This careful effort at community building through design was not lost on critics. Sum-
ming up the observations of many contemporary observers,

Figure 4.4. The houses of Mt. Washington near Chatham Village are single-family homes of various late-nineteenth and early-twentieth-century materials and designs.

Harold S. Buttenheim remarked in his magazine *The American City* that "Chatham Village is not merely a group of houses—it is a community of homes."[9] Marketing materials proclaimed and the tenants' social lives attested that Chatham Village was not just a place to live; it was a way of life.

Even the best construction and design could do only so much to ensure that the residents of the community would live by the principles upon which it had been planned. Property management thus became another important means by which the Buhl Foundation sought to control its tenants' environment and protect its investment. Lewis addressed this issue with characteristic vigor and attention to detail once the decision had been made to rent rather than sell the housing

Figure 4.5. The connected brick row houses of Chatham Village display a unified, altogether different design vocabulary.

units. Asserting that even the best-built housing development could not succeed without competent management, Lewis urged the foundation to seize the opportunity to command "a demonstration in management quite as unique and useful as the demonstration in community planning and house design."[10]

Lewis congratulated himself on "his" decision to rent instead of sell the homes at Chatham Village. By this time, he had thoroughly convinced himself that professionally managed rental housing was a real and viable alternative to families during the Depression, whose other housing options most frequently consisted of renting from an absentee landlord or financing the purchase of a cheaply built speculative house through an expensive second mortgage: "It is clearly apparent that under proper management a far greater degree of social, as well as economic, security can be had through tenancy than home ownership," Lewis wrote, with the conviction of the converted.[11] "Proper management" was assumed from the outset to mean management by the Buhl Foundation, since no one to whom the task could be delegated knew the project so well or had so great a stake in its success. With this in mind, Lewis laid out three broad principles to underlie Chatham Village's administration.

First, Lewis emphasized, the development was not philanthropic housing, and should never be regarded as such by either tenants or managers. That the foundation should, by word and deed, constantly underscore the commercial nature of its involvement in the project was a policy geared toward attracting the right kind of tenants. Having built the ideal place to live, the foundation now depended on the ideal community of residents to ensure its success: "sound, middle-class, white-collar folks who had achieved financial stability and who now wanted the social stability of just such a neighborhood of homes for their youngsters and themselves."[12]

Lewis warned against ever giving the impression that homes were to be rented for less than market value, for this would "attract the type of person who is always led to lean upon charity." He also admonished the Buhl Foundation to avoid the appearance that there was a ceiling on eligible income, lest "upstanding, self-respecting" tenants be frightened away by the thought that there was "an income tag upon residence in the Buhl Foundation's project."[13] Furthermore, tenants were never to know the basis upon which they had been selected, though to anyone of a critical mind, the demographics of the community served as a clear description of the entrance criteria. The Foundation's social planning at Chatham Village amounted to a blueprint for perfecting residential life by leaving much of it out. Chatham Village residents were overwhelmingly white, Protestant, mainstream, and middle-

class. Potential residents were subject to a highly personal interview with the on-premises manager and, in the days before
fair housing laws, African Americans, Jews, Catholics, homo-
sexuals, and others outside the dominant social milieu were
not admitted. Even dogs and cats were excluded, so as not to
disturb the delicate social balance that would ensure Chatham
Village's success. One tenant noted in 1938, "newcomers are apt
to be very much like (and usually friends of) established residents."[14] Even after moving in, strict social codes applied. Any
resident who displayed "deviant" behavior of any sort risked
being evicted.[15] Limiting residence to families of "quality" was
a tried and true formula for social and financial security. The
experimental aspects of Chatham Village were strictly limited
to its economics and planning.[16] When it came to tenant selection, the foundation was not taking any chances.

Second, Lewis believed that Chatham Village should be
administered as an investment, not as a speculative venture.
The investment motive, he reasoned, was more long-sighted
than the speculative motive, and therefore better geared to
the sense of "partnership" that was to characterize the relations between tenant and management at Chatham Village.[17]
Although the occupants of the project were renters, Lewis
wanted to discourage transience and foster a strong sense of
loyalty and pride—what might today be called "ownership"—
in the new community. Naturally, this was a two-way street.
In order for tenants to develop a lasting commitment to
Chatham Village, management would have to lead the way. In
place of a "'hard-shelled' commercial attitude" in dealing with
tenants, therefore, Lewis called for "a patient willingness to
drill back into the community" and "to work with a long
range purpose."[18] He admonished, however, that in order to
avoid exorbitant maintenance and depreciation costs, senti-
mentality must be avoided, especially in dealing with any de-
linquent tenant. Only by setting high standards and strictly
enforcing them would the foundation protect its investment
and the security of its tenant "partners."

Third, Lewis insisted that the key to making renters partners in the housing development was to foster community involvement and pride. This required two strategies on the part of the Buhl Foundation: it must select tenants with leadership qualities, and it must give them something to lead. To this end, Lewis proposed the establishment of a monthly community newsletter, "designed to furnish useful information to the tenants and appeal to their good will." Thus was born the *Chatham Village News*, which began publication in 1932, the year the first phase opened. The Buhl Foundation also agreed to tenants' requests to renovate the old Bigham mansion on the property as a headquarters for the Chatham Village Club, recognizing this tenant-formed organization as a boon to community cohesiveness and participation. Ever the entrepreneur, Lewis saw the intelligence and energy of Chatham Village's residents as a commodity to be capitalized upon to meet economic as well as social goals. Fortunately, the Buhl Foundation was in the position of having a long list of potential tenants from which to cull "a hand-picked community of persons of high social and intellectual standards."[19] Within a month after the opening of phase one, all 129 homes had been rented, and a sizable waiting list assured continued occupancy.

It was rare, however, for a unit to become available. From the outset, Chatham Village boasted an extremely low tenant turnover rate. Occupancy has never dropped below 97.5 percent and has hovered near 100 percent since 1936, with the unfilled fraction due only to brief periods of vacancy between tenants. During Chatham Village's first six years, the average length of residence was 4.35 years, with half the vacancies necessitated by business transfers and most of the rest brought about by residents building their own homes.

The loyalty of Chatham Village's tenants reflected Lewis's meticulous concern for their happiness, which, in turn, would guarantee his experiment's success. Lewis supervised every stage of the project personally, immersing himself in

Figure 4.6. "Country Fair Social" at Chatham Hall, 1938

the details to the point that the foundation office staff joked that he knew the exact location of every brick and stone. For Lewis, nothing was too good for his housing demonstration, so long as the improvements did not jeopardize a 4 percent return.[20]

To deal with the day-to-day duties of running Chatham Village, Lewis called for the foundation to form a subsidiary corporation, which came to be known as the Chatham Village Realty Company. Administered, capitalized, and chartered by the foundation, it leased the Chatham Village property from the parent organization and managed the Village from an office on the premises. Here tenants paid their rents to the company; the company then turned the checks over immediately to the foundation, which managed the proceeds and kept the books. Lewis expressed confidence that the large waiting list for homes would apply pressure on residents to stay current in their payments, and called for every aspect of tenant-management relations to be conducted in "utmost dignity" so that "the tenant may completely feel . . . that he is paying for what he gets."[21]

Conscientious, expert maintenance was perhaps the most important element of tenant satisfaction. Thus, Lewis required the site office manager to be "a man of practical experience in building, preferably a good carpenter," for he would need to perform routine repair and redecorating jobs. In addition, this superintendent would, with the help of a staff of one stenographer and one laborer, keep records of rent payments and repair requests as well as direct all lawn maintenance, outside cleaning, and interior renovation. For, Lewis wrote, "It is apparent that after the property is once filled the ordinary problem of rents and of collection will be the smallest part of the operating job. Physical maintenance of the property and the maintenance of proper community spirit are the more important and the more difficult phases of the project. They will be dependent first upon the establishment of wise governing principles by the Foundation and second upon the selection of the right type of man for the actual administration of the property on the ground."[22]

Lewis's concerted efforts to maintain the beauty of surroundings and quality of life at Chatham Village paid off in an extraordinary level of tenant satisfaction, as seen in consistently high occupancy rates, long waiting lists, and property value appreciation. In addition, the project showed a profit throughout the Depression and all the years the Buhl Foundation owned it (1932–1959), and it earned enduring praise for its expertly designed, extraordinarily pleasant environment.

Tenant testimony confirms what the statistics suggest:

Figure 4.7. Maintaining the Chatham Village landscape

early residents of Chatham Village were pleased with the community the Buhl Foundation had created.[23] Few were put off by the exclusivity or other restrictions of the meticulously controlled environment. On the contrary, after their experiences renting housing in the speculative market, many seemed to crave what the planned community had to offer. One early resident wrote: "Eight years of noisy apartments and dark houses, eight years of undignified but unavoidable squabbling with sluggish renting agents and over-thrifty landlords about leaking faucets and balky furnaces had made us wonder whether there was any hope for decent middle-class housing in Pittsburgh. Then came the promise . . . of a new kind of living."[24]

This resident and others adopted a practical approach to

Figure 4.8. Chatham Village children gathered in the sandbox during summer playschool, 1942

Figure 4.9. Village children doing crafts in the summer of 1932

life in the ideal community. To them, the paternalism of Lewis' management program was manifested most noticeably in Chatham Village's positive qualities: its conspicuous safety, punctual maintenance, community spirit, and low cost. Most of the early tenants were young couples with small children, and they liked knowing their youngsters were safe at the Chatham Village nursery school or playing in the interior courtyards, sandboxes, and paths.

With young families to raise and worry about, these resi-

Figure 4.10. A young villager peers into one of the streams in Chatham Wood on a snowy day in January 1941

Figure 4.11. A group of children exiting their nursery school in Chatham Hall, 1937

dents also appreciated being free from the time- and money-consuming tasks of home ownership or from dealing with irresponsible city slumlords. The same resident quoted above characterized the tenant-landlord relationship at Chatham Village as "striking" in contrast to that in her previous apartments. She wrote: "To residents accustomed to wrangling with renting agents for adequate heat in winter, for paint and wallpaper in the spring, and for plumbing repairs the year round, the village maintenance policy was like a pleasant dream following a nightmare. . . . Here, a phone call to the Village office was received with thanks, repairmen came promptly, and adjustments or replacements were made at once."[25] These comments were typical of residents interviewed, all of whom had a "great management" story to share.

Tenants also appreciated Chatham Village's close-knit community atmosphere, which was particularly pronounced during the lean years of the Depression and before television and air-conditioning kept more people entertained and comfortable indoors. Social clubs and traditions took hold quickly as residents, all drawn from the same stratum of society, tended to share many interests and customs in common. Since so many were young parents, a Mother's Club was one of the first organized social groups to form, followed by an arts and crafts club, dramatic society, and the Chatham Village Club, a general social, cultural, and recreational organization which is still extant. Sub-groups formed within this club to serve the various interests of its members, including music,

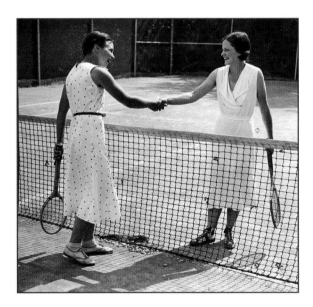

Figure 4.12. A game of tennis on Chatham Village courts, 1932

Figure 4.13. Annual Chatham Village Easter egg hunt, 1938

Figure 4.14. A photography club exhibit in Chatham Hall, 1937

bridge, photography, woodworking, child study, and reading. The club also sponsored parties, teas, dances, tournaments, trips, and holiday events such as Christmas caroling and Easter egg hunts. Moreover, the amenities of Chatham Village came at a discount. Due to the limited-dividend nature of the financing, rental prices were kept artificially low, and the Buhl Foundation actually lowered rather than raised rents to keep its tenants through the depths of the Depression.

In 1956, Charles Lewis retired as director of the Buhl Foundation. His successor, Dr. Charles B. Nutting, decided that the Buhl Foundation's experiment in housing had reached a successful conclusion.[26] Nutting contacted the Foundation for Cooperative Housing (FCH), a nonprofit organization dedicated to encouraging cooperative housing in the interests of the consumer, of which Clarence Stein was a member. Convinced of the merits of cooperative home ownership, Nutting entered into negotiations regarding the sale of Chatham Village to the FCH, which would buy the property on behalf of the tenants and sell it to them in turn. "The Buhl Foundation has been interested for some time in giving residents of Chatham Village the opportunity to own their own homes," Nutting remarked. "We believe that this plan offers the best chance of success."[27] The Buhl Foundation was willing to sell Chatham Village at the cost of its total investment, and to accept only a 3 percent down payment of $60,000 from the FCH. Closing the deal depended on the willingness of the Federal Housing Administration to insure the mortgage.

Chatham Village's conversion from a rental community to a corporation of resident members was accomplished under the cooperative provisions of the National Housing Act. The Federal Housing Administration accepted the FCH's application under the 1959 amendments to Section 213 of the act, which allow the agency to guarantee 97 percent of the mortgage on cooperatives formed out of existing properties. In Chatham Village's case, this was the full 97 percent of $2.2 million, the Buhl Foundation's total investment plus transfer and administrative costs to run the community for forty years. The deal made history, as Chatham Village was the first property to be sold for cooperative housing under the 1959 amendments.

Chatham Village tenants, who packed meetings at the local junior high school to learn about the transfer, were told that they would be given thirty-day first options to buy their own homes. David Krooth, an official with the FCH, told residents that he was "extremely anxious that everyone now living in Chatham Village be given the chance to buy. If a family

Figure 4.15. Inside Chatham Village today

needs special consideration, we'll work out a plan for them."
Nutting assured them that, in all likelihood, "Every family in
the Village will be able to share in the project at a monthly
cost to them below what they are now paying." Such favorable
terms were possible because of the Buhl Foundation's decision
to sell at cost. With down payments of $300 to $500, depending on the size of the dwelling, the cost of a share in the new
cooperative compared favorably to the cost of renting in
Chatham Village or other middle-class Pittsburgh locales.[28]

Given the choice of buying into the co-op or moving out
of Chatham Village, only 4 of 216 families elected to move.

The rest of Chatham Village's former tenants formed a cooperative corporation, Chatham Village Homes, Inc., to own and administer the community. This corporation held one title to the entire property, including buildings and land, and the title was divided into 216 shares—one per living unit. Each share was represented by a certificate of membership, giving a resident the right to live in a certain unit, to use the communal grounds and facilities, and to be a participating member of the corporation. Each unit was assigned a book value according to the home's size, and that value increased a set amount per year, with equity accumulating in the unit. Chatham Village Homes, Inc., was organized as a par value cooperative, meaning that the corporation assumed responsibility for the transfer of dwelling units from one owner to another. That is, when a member chose to vacate a dwelling, he or she sold his or her certificate of membership back to the corporation, which in turn sold it to the next incoming resident. Beyond the increase in the book value of the membership, there was no profit to the resident. The corporation's rules specifically prohibited speculative dealings. When a member improved an individual house, the value the improvement added to that member's equity was decreased each succeeding year so that, over time, all units of the same size—whether improved or not—maintained roughly the same value.[29]

The membership elected a board of directors to administer the corporation's policies. Residents financed the mortgage and maintenance of Chatham Village through monthly payments, which varied according to the size of their units. Part of each payment to the corporation went toward the owner's equity in his or her home. Since the mortgage was insured by the Department of Housing and Urban Development, this agency also served in an authoritative capacity regarding major policy decisions and revisions.

The responsibility for home maintenance now shifted to the residents. To moderate the expense of general upkeep, the corporation decided that residents should maintain the interiors of their own units with respect to routine care and redecoration, including painting or refinishing of walls, woodwork, and floors. Remodeling of kitchens and bathrooms became an individual option. Maintenance involving structural features, plumbing and heating equipment, and electrical installations, however, remained the responsibility of Chatham Village Homes, which also oversaw the continued care of landscaping and grounds.

The high percentage of residents who chose to stay in Chatham Village after its sale helped assure continuity in the transition from rental housing to cooperative corporation. The corporation sold the few vacated units to families on the waiting list, which was longer than that for any other residential community or apartment complex in Pittsburgh. The chance that conversion to cooperative ownership would make Chatham Village accessible to "outsiders" was, in the words of one newspaper reporter, "extremely dim."[30]

Though a fundamental departure from its original scheme, Chatham Village's transition to cooperative ownership did not have a dramatic effect on either the physical form or the social life of the community. Unlike most urban neighborhoods of similar vintage, which have ridden waves of popularity and decline, Chatham Village has consistently thrived as a middle-class haven. Its remarkable stability can be attributed to a number of factors, including sound initial planning, design, and construction, and the suitability of cooperative ownership to Chatham Village's original development.

Despite the rhetoric of "economic democracy" espoused by Lewis, Stein, and Wright, their planned community has benefited from being an intentional enclave. Original tenants noted their affinity to their Chatham Village neighbors and weak social connection to Mt. Washington as a whole, while today's cooperative residents liken their membership to life on a college campus. The Chatham Village Club, to which every member belongs, is an apt metaphor for the nature of life in the community. "There is no public life here, in any city sense," observed urban critic Jane Jacobs. "There are differing degrees of extended private life." Regarding the community's insularity, she continued: "Chatham Village's success as a 'model' neighborhood where much is shared has required that the residents be similar to one another in their standards, interests and backgrounds. . . . It has also required that residents set themselves distinctly apart from the different people in the surrounding city; these are in the main also middle class, but lower middle class, and this is too different for the degree of chumminess that neighborliness in Chatham Village entails." Jacobs noted the practical consequences of being an island. Faced with the need to cooperate with residents of different neighborhoods in a matter at the local public school, she reported, the parents of Chatham Village found that there was "no public acquaintanceship, no foundation of casual public trust, no cross-connections with the necessary people—and no practice or ease in applying the most ordinary techniques of city public life at lowly levels."[31]

Built for clerical workers, Chatham Village quickly became home to a variety of middle-income professionals—lawyers, teachers, architects, junior executives, even players of professional sports. Though the economic strata of today's residents is roughly the same as, if not slightly wealthier than, that of early tenants, the diversity of races and cultures has grown, while that of ages has narrowed.[32] The first tenants were primarily young families; old photographs and articles about the Village prominently feature small children playing together in sandboxes and on playground equipment, or safely riding tricycles on traffic-free paths. Residents ran a nursery school in the Chatham Hall clubhouse, and teenagers fielded tennis teams. A 1960 retrospective article in *Architectural Forum* reported that a "good handful of children born and raised in the Village have grown up, married, and returned to raise their own children there."[33] This can no longer be said. For many years, the consequence of the low turnover rate was that the median age of the population tended to climb as its residents stayed on. By 1980, a *Post-Gazette* article included an estimate that as many as two-thirds of residents were well into their fifties or older.[34] In the 1990s, a new generation of young people moved in, but tended to be single professionals or childless couples. Although the shared amenities of Chatham Village offer a safe, pleasant, sociable setting for parents and children, the size of the houses is small by the standards of the modern middle-class family, which tends to require separate bedrooms for each child as well as other, specialized spaces such as home offices and exercise rooms. Recently, a small baby boom has been observed in Chatham Village, but in comparison to its early days, the community is no longer home to many children. By 1993, the population of children in Chatham Village had dwindled to the point that the nursery school closed. Today, sandboxes remain, but tricycles and teenage social life are rarely seen. In response to an urban public school system perceived as troubled, many residents move to the suburbs when their children near school age; some move back when their children have grown.[35] In this respect, the most careful planning within Chatham Village has not successfully shielded it from the problems of the city at large.

While broader changes in American housing patterns and preferences have factored in the demographic shifts at Chatham Village, the change in the community's ownership structure has not. In fact, cooperative ownership has tended to perpetuate the physical and social controls that ensured the community's original success. In 1931, Frederick Bigger, asked by Charles Lewis to participate in the early stages of the housing project's planning, described cooperative ownership as a means to ensure the permanence of Chatham Village's amenities. Before they had even been built, Bigger wrote that Chatham Village's common grounds and facilities "should be kept in common for all the houses and [their] maintenance properly provided for. This means that individual houses need not necessarily be sold. A purchaser would, instead, buy a proportionate interest in the whole development, sufficient to entitle him to live in one of the dwellings and to contribute a proportionate share for the maintenance of the gardens and their amenities."[36] Thirty years later, Bigger's words proved prescient in their description of how cooperative ownership actually would work to preserve the most distinctive, idyllic, and potentially fragile aspects of the physical community, as well as its social stability. Another form of resident ownership—for instance, a condominium-type system—would have destroyed the integrity of the Chatham Village plan by breaking up its single ownership. Chatham Village was, after all, built to demonstrate the virtues of large-scale residential planning; it is only appropriate that its ownership be on the scale of the entire community. In addition, the ownership of shares of the whole instead of individual physical spaces makes it possible to retain the communal aspects of the Village so essential to its original plan: the courtyards, recreational areas, greenbelt and Chatham Hall still belong to all residents in almost exactly equal measure.

Cooperative ownership also harkens back to Ebenezer Howard's search for an economic structure to harmonize the interests of the individual and the community, tenant and landlord. Howard realized that a form of land ownership that gave collective rights and responsibilities to residents themselves would be effective in maintaining the quality of the built environment for the benefit of all, and Unwin linked this idea with the emerging English "co-partnership" movement, founded by Henry Vivian, which held that housing was about more than individual dwellings, and common ownership of land and buildings was the ideal means of linking the physical aspects of a site with its communal life.[37]

The transfer of ownership from the Buhl Foundation to the residents' corporation perpetuated coherence of policy as well as unity of design; coherent management from without was simply transferred to coherent management from within. The main difference is that now, instead of protecting the

Buhl Foundation's investment, Chatham Village members protect their own. Chatham Village's corporation has elected officials and four committees—house, grounds, membership, and security—which, like municipal agencies, craft policy and adjudicate disputes on various aspects of life in the community. Of these, the membership and house committees bear the greatest responsibility for perpetuating the ideals on which Chatham Village was built.

The membership committee screens and chooses new residents of Chatham Village. Whereas the Buhl Foundation had selected its ideal tenants, in 1960 the membership committee began selecting its ideal neighbors. That the Buhl Foundation's selection policies were acceptable to its former tenants is evident in the stability of the community's population even after its transition from foundation to cooperative management. The committee's broad freedom to pick and choose prospective buyers into the co-op was drastically curtailed by the Fair Housing Act of 1968 and its subsequent amendments.[38] Today, the membership committee's role consists of conducting interviews with prospective tenants in which expectations and obligations of membership in the planned community are emphasized. The Fair Housing Act prohibits discrimination on the basis of race, age, gender, religion, and other factors of a personal nature. But to live in Chatham Village, one still must be financially responsible and socially committed to life in a planned community. Thus, in their self-appointed responsibility for screening their prospective neighbors, members of Chatham Village Homes, Inc., retain a little of the Buhl Foundation's control over the socioeconomic makeup of the community.

The house committee has translated the Buhl Foundation's architectural and design values to a set of policies the residents now enforce for themselves. Members have chosen to uphold the Buhl Foundation's investment in quality materials and design, and have thus scarcely altered the physical aspects of the community. A passage from the Chatham Village members' handbook reads, "Preserving the distinctive architectural features of our site and buildings helps to protect property values and each member's investment."

There is some truth in criticisms of Chatham Village as an intentionally homogenous, insular, middle-class island. The Buhl Foundation created this enclave to ensure the social and economic success of its housing demonstration, and the structure of cooperative ownership has perpetuated the cozy feeling of living in a private club. On the other hand, the integrity of the planned community over eighty years of social, managerial, and technological change is testament to its extraordinary success in serving the needs of its residents and owners.

five   **A Demonstration, Not a Revolution**

In 1955, Charles Lewis declared that the Buhl Foundation's objectives for Chatham Village "have been fully realized."[1] Lewis's claim was in some regards an overstatement, but Chatham Village was extraordinarily successful: high occupancy rates, low tenant turnover, and long waiting lists for units have been steady characteristics of the community since the day it opened in 1932. Through economic depression, war, and inflation, the community continued to bring

133

the Buhl Foundation a stable annual return in excess of 4 percent until it was sold to its tenants in 1960. Catherine Bauer lauded Chatham Village as "probably the best example of modern planned housing in the country."[2] Yet despite its self-contained success, Lewis's experiment did not succeed in revolutionizing residential design in America. In the initial flurry of enthusiasm surrounding its construction, a few imitations were built, but nothing approaching the large-scale replication its creators envisioned and expected.

Today, Chatham Village's secluded site and an unspoken understanding among its residents conspire to make it one of the best-kept housing secrets in Pittsburgh. But, especially in the first ten years after its construction, Chatham Village was anything but obscure. The swiftness with which residents rented units and the fact that the housing plan made money for the Buhl Foundation caught the attention of business executives and investors, while the succinct elegance of its design led the emerging public housing movement to cite it as an exemplar of what good housing could be. Tenants and critics alike extolled the planned community's amenities, and few disagreed that it was a desirable place to live. From the announcement of the Buhl Foundation's plans through the start of World War II, Chatham Village was a celebrated as a model and inspiration for architects, planners, developers, and investors.

Its renown must largely be attributed to the inexhaustible efforts of Charles Lewis to advocate for the Chatham Village model and the ability of private capital to solve America's slum-housing crisis. Lewis hired a public relations firm to promote the demonstration project and called upon his own skills as a newspaper editor to campaign for a favorable public response.[3] He commissioned models and a motion picture of Chatham Village and toured conferences with them. Whenever possible, Lewis recruited Clarence Stein and Henry Wright to join him in personally addressing delegates on the virtues of planned communities.

The most prominent and influential of these conferences

Figure 5.1. A plaster model of Chatham Village

was Herbert Hoover's President's Conference on Home Building and Home Ownership held in December 1931. Delegates at this gathering paid considerable attention to Stein and Wright's plans for Radburn as well as for Chatham Village. They focused not only on the innovative design and attractive amenities of these communities, but on the economics of large-scale operations and planning housing in groups that allowed them to be built economically and efficiently. As a result, the final recommendations of the conference were favorable toward the construction of large-scale, comprehensively planned communities of grouped rental housing and detached, owner-occupied dwellings alike.

No matter how persuasive the model, though, few private

investors were in a position to become large-scale, limited-dividend developers as the Depression continued to worsen. Instead, the federal government began to assume a greater and greater role in housing, providing subsidies for public apartment projects as well as mortgage insurance for single-family homes. The idea of public assistance in housing deeply disturbed Charles Lewis, who feared that the government's intention to interfere with the production of housing heralded the dawn of socialism. He repositioned his promotional campaign of Chatham Village accordingly, representing the community as a righteous symbol of private capital's ability to meet the housing needs of the nation without courting the perils of public landlordism.

The most ringing endorsement of the Chatham Village demonstration—and a direct outcome of its influence at the President's Conference on Home Building and Home Ownership—was, in fact, the large-scale rental housing program of the Federal Housing Administration, established by the National Housing Act of 1934. By setting a framework for government-insured mortgage loans and setting national standards for large-scale neighborhood design, the FHA backed the private construction of planned communities for moderate-income families based on the models of Radburn and Chatham Village. The provision of mortgage security, an important component of the RPAA's community-building vision, supplied the confidence sought by banks and other investors and served as a catalyst for the moribund commercial building industry.[4]

The FHA's policies encouraged large-scale development by an "operative builder" who managed everything: financing and land acquisition; site and building design; and hiring architects, landscape architects, engineers, and tradespeople to carry out the work. FHA architect Henry Klaber, who was instrumental in drawing up the FHA's standards for architecture and subdivision design, was a close friend and former classmate of Clarence Stein's and a founding member of the

RPAA. His influence ensured that FHA standards strongly favored the RPAA's model of American garden city planning. As a result, exemplified features such as superblocks, attached dwellings grouped around landscaped courtyards, and integral community amenities, including commercial buildings, playgrounds, and parks, became the basis for mortgage insurance and loan approval of many large-scale housing developments planned and built in the 1930s.[5]

One of the first communities to be realized under the new FHA regulations was Buckingham Village, developed by operative builder Allie S. Freed, a New York real estate promoter with wealth, skill, and strong financial contacts. In 1935, with plans of Chatham Village supplied by Charles Lewis and with Henry Wright in charge of site planning, Freed applied the mass production techniques of the automobile industry to the construction of a rental garden-apartment complex for 1,014 families in Arlington, Virginia, a suburb of Washington, D.C. Buckingham was closely followed by other planned garden apartment communities designed in direct imitation of Chatham Village, including Colonial Village, also in Arlington; Baldwin Hills Village, designed by Clarence Stein in Los Angeles; and Hancock Village in Boston.

Freed also organized the Committee on Economic and Social Progress, Inc., an honorary advisory board to endorse the idea of mass-produced, limited-dividend housing projects patterned after Chatham Village. As a member of the board, Charles Lewis proclaimed that Buckingham promised to be the most significant housing demonstration ever undertaken (though, ultimately, Buckingham surpassed Chatham Village only in scale; neither its character as affordable rental housing nor its original site plan have been maintained intact). Lewis envisioned the creation of a national housing corporation as the next step, but the billion-dollar enterprise was not to be. Freed's untimely death and the collapse of the brief economic boom put an end to these plans before they began.[6]

Beyond the regulatory framework of the FHA, there were

other notable campaigns by Lewis's supporters to expand upon the Buhl Foundation's model. One of these was a scheme by Joseph Catherine, Walter S. Schmidt, and Paul E. Stark, president and former presidents of the National Association of Real Estate Boards. The cornerstone of their plan was a billion-dollar national organization that would coordinate a program for the housing industry by pooling purchasing power and real estate and architectural abilities. Their costs thus lowered, local "realty factors" would be able to build a billion dollars' worth of housing—patterned, of course, after Chatham Village—within five years. The idea was backed by numerous realtors willing to organize local mortgage associations, but in the end there was not a critical mass of support large enough to move the ambitious plan past the publicity stage.[7]

Chatham Village also influenced the housing programs of major life insurance companies. In announcing the Metropolitan Life Insurance Company's intention to invest $100 million in low-cost, modern, planned apartment communities in 1938, chairman of the board Frederick H. Ecker praised the Buhl Foundation's demonstration for awakening private capital to its social responsibilities and for its constant campaign against government encroachment on the housing responsibilities of private enterprise. The rental-housing complexes Metropolitan Life built in New York City—Parkchester, Stuyvesant Town, Peter Cooper Village, and Riverton Houses, all still extant—demonstrate the relationship of Stein and Wright's economical model of low-density New Town planning to early American experiments with "towers in the park," designed according to European-influenced Modernist ideals to provide affordable housing and open space in an urban setting. Built in one of the densest cities in the world, the Metropolitan Life communities are superblocks of high-rise apartment buildings set amid central greens and tree-lined pedestrian paths, intended to allow New Yorkers to "live in a park."[8] Though Clarence Stein continued to advocate low-rise, decentralized communities over high-rise inner-city housing, he endorsed Metropolitan Life's investment in these apartments, declaring in 1940 that their management by a single owner would protect their park-like amenities and that, through their large-scale planning, "all the waste of the old speculative system has been eliminated."[9]

At the end of World War II, the John Hancock Life Insurance Company initiated construction of Hancock Village, a $12 million garden apartment community on a former golf course in the Boston suburb of Brookline. Developed as rental units to house returned veterans and their families, Hancock Village consists of 789 attached, two-story units in 55 buildings set amid landscaped courtyards designed by the renowned local firm of Olmsted Associates. As at Chatham Village, the living areas of Hancock Village homes face onto its interior courtyards, and the community was designed to include practical amenities such as garage compounds, recreation facilities, and a shopping center.[10]

Despite these stirrings toward large-scale community building influenced by the planning ideals of the RPAA, Lewis and his supporters—mostly real estate professionals who resented the government's intrusion into their economic territory—ultimately were not successful in their campaign to reeducate and revolutionize the private building industry. FHA incentives notwithstanding, relatively few real estate investors showed initiative, and popular and political pressure for a full federal housing program mounted steadily. In 1937, Congress passed the United States Housing Act (also called the Wagner-Steagall Act), coauthored by Catherine Bauer, establishing the U.S. Housing Authority with a budget of $20 million and the power to make loans totaling $500 million. By the end of 1939, nineteen public housing projects had been constructed in thirteen cities, and the maximum funds had been approved as loans for use in 155 communities.[11] In 1941, the nation's entrance into World War II diverted its housing reform energies, and Chatham Village's initial window of influence slammed shut.

The main reason that the vast majority of builders failed to organize limited-dividend development companies is self-evident: returns were limited, usually to about 6 percent. In addition, large-scale building required considerable investment capital up front, which builders were loath to commit during depressed economic times. The investment of effort and expertise to successfully plan and build a Chatham Village was also more than the building industry, grown comfortable in its speculative habits, wanted to take on. The old speculative model of development was tried, true, and relatively fast to turn a profit. All of these factors hindered a culture change within the building industry, particularly during the declining markets of the Depression and World War II.

Even Clarence Stein was pessimistic. In a letter to his wife in 1936, he wrote of a conversation with Frederick Bigger in which the Pittsburgh planner raised the question of "the prospects of building more private capital [residential projects] like Radburn and Chatham Village." Stein replied, "I find it difficult to advise people to do so on an investment basis, because how can we tell what will happen in thirty years? There certainly will probably be no interest in investment without interest."[12]

In 1938, *Architectural Record* published an article entitled "Large-Scale Housing: Its Past, Its New Status, Its Problems, Its Possibilities," which examined "the mass production Idea [*sic*] applied to home building." The magazine's editors offered a cautious endorsement of the Chatham Village demonstration and the planned rental communities built on its model, noting, "that it will work and work successfully in isolated instances has been demonstrated over and over again." However, while recognizing the need for "housing midway between the ceiling of Government subsidized projects and what has heretofore been regarded as the floor for private enterprise"—the very market to which Chatham Village was aimed—the article qualified its prediction that the Buhl Foundation's demonstration could become the default model for moderate-income housing development: "Whether it can will depend on two things: its ability to attract sponsors and capital, and to reach and satisfy a market."[13]

The market, it turned out, could be satisfied with a lesser product than Chatham Village, and the building industry was content to supply just what the market demanded and no more. With the conservative building business unconvinced, the most progressive supporters of the Buhl Foundation's demonstration also fell away. Frederick Ackerman—who, as the most radical of the RPAA members, believed that no meaningful change could occur within the exploitative framework of capitalism—ceased promoting the garden city model of development when he concluded that attempts to graft its essentially communitarian land-use planning principles onto America's conventional free-market system were futile. Building a community such as Sunnyside, Radburn, or Chatham Village required the backing of supportive government policy, the implementation of a common form of property ownership to keep housing prices affordable, and the luxury of a long lead time to allow for comprehensive planning.[14] After World War II, when the near-dormant building industry revived to meet the pressing need to house returning GIs and their families, builders who took years to conduct sociological and site-planning studies before breaking ground risked losing out on the boom. In the rush to meet the pent-up demand, abstract ideas of social enlightenment were left largely on the drawing boards. Ackerman's doubts proved prophetic, and Levittown, not Chatham Village, became the large-scale prototype for the postwar housing boom. To an extent, this also served to ratify Charles Lewis's early conviction that housing consumers held a strong preference for traditional, detached single-family homes, along with conventional street frontage and private yards.

The Chatham Village demonstration proved that limited-dividend housing could be built in an innovative manner and rented to make a profit, and it inspired the planning and construction of several communities in its image across the United States, but in the end these accomplishments were not enough to cause a social revolution in the private building industry. Moreover, neither Chatham Village nor its tireless booster, Charles Lewis, could block the federal government from becoming involved with the desperately needed low-income housing programs that private builders would not undertake on their own. Even Chatham Village itself stopped short of serving those most needy of well-built, well-planned housing.

It is hardly surprising that such an ambitious goal could not be realized by one community or one man, even the director of an influential foundation. When the Depression finally ended, the building industry found itself newly hampered by the production constraints of World War II, and the problem of housing low-income families continued to fall largely to the government to solve. Pittsburgh urban historian Roy Lubove has harshly concluded that Chatham Village demonstrated not the potential, but the bankruptcy of voluntarism as a strategy for housing reform.[15] Others have taken a more balanced view. Donald Lisio, author of a study of the Buhl Foundation, summed up Chatham Village's influence by pointing out that "although the Buhl Foundation failed to stimulate a major national reform movement in housing, it did demonstrate how private capital, through experimentation, could contribute to the development of a reasonable and promising solution to a pressing national problem."[16]

That Chatham Village was influential is indisputable. In the 1930s, every architect and planner with access to professional publications knew of its existence through detailed articles, plans, and photographs. Its large-scale planning, grouped housing, car-free courtyards, and greenbelt supplied the very vocabulary of residential site design during the Great Depression. Its earliest imitators, such as Buckingham, were celebrated, too, as evidence that a new housing paradigm had taken hold.

Ultimately, though, it had not. The proliferation of the Chatham Village idea was never as successful—or as well documented—as Chatham Village itself. The garden-style housing developed in response to the Buhl Foundation's demonstration was lesser, often in every regard, than the source of its inspiration: in scale, in investment, in innovative treatments of buildings, sites, and amenities. Stein and Wright's followers never achieved the brilliance, and therefore the renown, of Stein and Wright themselves. This makes the true extent of Chatham Village's lineage difficult to establish. Literally untold numbers of places were developed according to its prototype in the 1930s and 1940s, but most of these have since faded quietly into obscurity, their connection to the ideals of Depression-era housing reform forgotten. In the eloquence of its expression of those ideals, Chatham Village remains the original, without peer.

Interest in the Buhl Foundation's demonstration was perhaps most intense in western Pennsylvania. Not only was housing reform here an urgent local concern, but Pittsburgh area planners' knowledge of Chatham Village was intimate and three-dimensional. Their ability to walk the celebrated footpaths and experience the Village in person made its example all the more immediate and compelling. Furthermore, the fact that Chatham Village had been built on Mt. Washington left no room for excuses. No one could say that it couldn't work here.

Though the construction industry in and around Pittsburgh, as elsewhere, ground nearly to a standstill during the Depression, several nearby communities were built during this time that incorporated the planning principles of Chatham Village. Although this occurred to varying extents and with different degrees of success, these western Pennsylvania places represent the impact of the Chatham Village model of residential design when and where it was at its strongest.

Dover Gables, built in 1936 in the Shadyside neighborhood of Pittsburgh, a streetcar suburb more upscale than

Mt. Washington, consists of forty Tudor Revival row houses in four rows aligned perpendicular, rather than parallel, to a major thoroughfare, so that instead of traffic, they face narrow greens accessible by pedestrian walkways. As at Chatham Village, a separate garage complex houses the residents' automobiles. Yet the small, constrained site—one block wide and less than one block long—does not allow for the spaciousness found at Chatham Village, nor were its natural contours used to advantage in the buildings' unimaginative site planning. Built on a fraction of the scale of Chatham Village, Dover Gables has a far more dense building-to-landscape ratio and lacks the private streets, curvilinear boundaries, park-like atmosphere, and greenbelt buffer that are essential to Chatham Village's suburban feel. It is also too small to include the commercial or recreational amenities that make Chatham Village a self-contained enclave. Indeed, tucked as it is into a conventional city block, Dover Gables integrates more successfully into the larger neighborhood than does its predecessor on Mt. Washington. Although its ownership structure is that of single-family homes, Dover Gables has, like Chatham Village, been well preserved, probably due to a combination of its aesthetic appeal—the houses' garden orientation make them a unique choice among row houses in Pittsburgh's East End—and its highly desirable location.

A more faithful and equally well-preserved copy of Chatham Village was developed in 1939–1940 by insurance executive Florence Biggert Jr., as rental housing in Crafton, a leafy suburb just west of Pittsburgh. Biggert Manor features seventeen units of attached dwellings in four rows which, like Chatham Village, are terraced on a steep hillside site. Two of the rows, sited back-to-back, have integral garages accessed from an adjacent city street, while two garage courts serve the remaining units. Biggert Manor's Colonial Revival–style architecture, designed by Schwab, Palmgreen & Associates, closely replicates that of Chatham Village, as do the stone retaining walls and meandering paths and staircases that pro-

Figure 5.2. Dover Gables in Pittsburgh, Pennsylvania

vide pedestrian circulation into and within the site. However, due to the small number of units and rows, there is only one true courtyard, and this is lined, rather than enclosed, by buildings. Another difference between this development and its predecessor is that Biggert Manor's perimeter is defined by public streets, with one private access drive in to the garage courts; therefore, its separation of pedestrian and automobile traffic is incomplete. There is also no true greenbelt, although the steepest corner of the site has been left wooded, in contrast to the more cultivated landscape in the rest of the development. Like Dover Gables, Biggert Manor contains no commercial or recreational facilities and is much smaller than Chatham Village in scale. Yet of all the Pittsburgh-area developments to respond to the Buhl Foundation's demonstration, Biggert Manor, with its dynamic site planning and thoughtful relationship between architecture and landscape design, is closest in spirit to its predecessor.

Located in New Kensington, eighteen miles northeast of Pittsburgh, Aluminum City Terrace combines the influence of Chatham Village with the later imprint of European Modernism. As the 1930s advanced, so did the ideas of progressive planners, housing reformers, and RPAA members such as Catherine Bauer, Robert Kohn, and Frederick Ackerman. They had become intrigued with German Bauhaus architecture, in which form famously followed function, and by the Radiant City planning of Le Corbusier, in which widely spaced, Modernist, high-rise apartment buildings—grouped housing on an oversized, vertical scale—were set in vast superblocks of open space. This parkland would replace the congested urban street grid, offering pleasant walking routes for pedestrians while expressways diverted cars. Though its underlying ideal was not dissimilar to that of Howard's and Unwin's garden city, Le Corbusier's Radiant City was markedly different in its dramatic scale, rigidly orthogonal layout, and severe, slab-like architectural expression. Through the efforts of the Depression-era housers to bring avant-garde European

Figure 5.3. Biggert Manor in Crafton, Pennsylvania

ideas to bear upon the persistent American problem of housing, garden city planning ideals of low-rise homes and businesses clustered within parkland became intermingled with an austere, authoritarian, modern aesthetic. Intellectuals of the period viewed fanciful architectural styles as tainted by association with the overindulgent boom that preceded the Great Depression, and looked to the "uncluttered" spaces and surfaces of European modernism as holding promise for housing low-income, working, and even middle-class families in the United States.

Designed by Walter Gropius and his protégé Marcel Breuer, German Bauhaus architects who had emigrated to the United States during World War II, Aluminum City was funded by the United States government in 1941 as wartime

Figure 5.4. Aluminum City Terrace in New Kensington, Pennsylvania

housing for workers in the development's namesake industry. The Federal Works Administration (FWA), which sought to influence workers' and their families' enduring housing preferences by exposing them to life in a planned Modernist community, deliberately chose to build Aluminum City Terrace in the International Style.[17] Federal officials intended their defense housing projects to be lasting contributions to the housing stock in their communities and to serve as models for postwar urban development.[18] While these planners considered multiunit dwellings and modern architecture suitable for industrial workers, they endeavored to balance the buildings' austere design with the livability of the communities in which they were built. As articulated by its American practi-

tioners, garden city theory held that grouped housing and
shared amenities would foster a social and civic life among
residents that would help sustain the American value of democracy. This point was not lost on planners during wartime.
The Bauhaus plan proposed by Gropius and Breuer provoked
vigorous criticism—particularly from New Kensington
realtor-turned-mayoral candidate W. C. Wally, who called the
buildings "chicken coops"—but the FWA's planners and their
architects prevailed.[19]

At Aluminum City Terrace, 250 attached homes in thirty-
five structures are arrayed to take advantage of southern ex-
posure on a high hilltop site of forty-three acres; a winding
public street snakes through the development, providing access to parking in several communal lots. Because the solar
orientation of the buildings dominates the site plan, there is
no other discernable art or geometry to their placement.
Rows may front streets, parking lots, or open spaces, which
are dispersed throughout the site. Buildings, too, are dispersed in a formation much looser than at Chatham Village;
no attempt has been made to foster smaller groupings within
the neighborhood by designing enclosed outdoor spaces. Accordingly, pedestrian circulation through the development
varies among conventional sidewalks, interior pathways, and
the temptation to shortcut across parking lots or communal
lawns.

Gropius and Breuer designed the buildings at Aluminum
City Terrace in their trademark International Style, which is
to say, with absolutely minimal decorative detail. Units may
be one or two stories in height, but all buildings are the same
length, limiting the variation possible in their siting. Further,
none is stepped or terraced, despite the rolling contours of the
site. A community building is available for rental, and a kin-
dergarten building that originally served the development's
children now functions as the Aluminum City Terrace Housing Association office.

The federal government sold Aluminum City Terrace in

1948 under the terms of a Mutual Home Ownership Plan,
which was the outcome of a protracted political battle over
the fate of the federal government's defense housing projects
after the war. Political liberals supported the conversion of
those structures to low-income housing, while conservatives
called for them to be sold on the open market. Under the
plan, residents who had been renting their homes from the
government, formed a not-for-profit housing association to
purchase their communities outright. Residents then purchased shares in the association, and the communities functioned as co-ops. This, officials believed, offered the best
means of providing housing assistance to families who neither qualified for low-income public housing nor had the
means to purchase their own homes on the open market.[20]

The Aluminum City Terrace Housing Association's rules
concerning the preservation of its original character are far
more lax than those at Chatham Village. The association has
initiated many significant, community-wide changes, such as
wholesale replacement of windows and other features. Vertical, stained cedar siding, which suggested a certain rusticity
when the buildings were built, has been replaced or painted
over, while distinctive slanted entrance canopies, which were
part of the original design, have been replaced throughout
with more conventional aluminum awnings. Other changes,
such as the enclosure and landscaping of individual yards,
vary greatly from household to household, and have served to
soften and personalize the development's original austere,
repetitive design.

In the same year that Aluminum City Terrace was built,
Clarence Stein designed three defense housing projects,
located in the Pittsburgh suburbs of Shaler, Stowe, and
Clairton. Of those, the communities in Shaler and Stowe
were built, and only the former, Shalercrest, survives. Other
than a few passing references in his correspondence, however,
Stein's foray into defense housing design is an obscure chapter in his history. The fact that he chose to omit these proj-

ects from his 1951 retrospective of his planning career, *To-ward New Towns for America*, suggests that he considered them outside of the evolution of his core New Town planning ideas. Practical constraints surely limited what Stein as able to accomplish at these sites. Yet, he wrote to his wife Aline of his work on them, "We are doing some new things. I am learning."[21]

Shalercrest demonstrates much about Stein's approach to the defense housing projects. There, 251 units in fifty-eight plain brick buildings are arrayed along a serpentine road as it climbs a rugged hillside. The street connects to the regular plan of the suburban township at both ends, defining an essentially linear plan for the project. Because the street existed before Shalercrest was developed, the creation of superblocks there was not possible. But Stein did add one cul-de-sac and one short spur street that leads to a parking lot before continuing as a sidewalk lined with buildings. In a more explicit, if not poetic, reference to Chatham Village, at a few points in the development, he organized buildings around "courts" accessed via pedestrian paths leading away from the road in straight lines or loops. Otherwise, however, pedestrian circulation within Shalercrest occurs via conventional sidewalks that follow the vehicular street. Siting of the buildings along the street is informal; while a few face the road directly, many are placed at assorted angles to it, creating more complex streetscapes and variations in the size and shape of interstitial green spaces. Landscape designer Ralph Griswold, who had worked with Stein on Chatham Village, did so again at Shalercrest.

Parking at Shalercrest is concentrated in several surface lots distributed throughout the plan. A park and playground are located in small vale, which is embraced by one of the U-shaped curves of the street. The development also includes a community building and a management and maintenance building, both still functional.

Buildings in Shalercrest vary from one to two-and-a-half

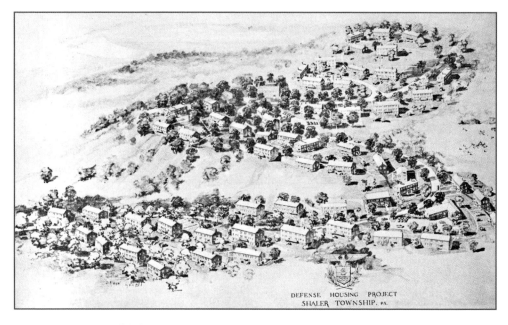

DEFENSE HOUSING PROJECT
SHALER TOWNSHIP, PA.

Figure 5.5. A rendering of Shalercrest, Shaler, Pennsylvania, designed by Clarence Stein

stories in height, but are of uniform length, whether they contain two, four, or six units. By keeping the length short, Stein was able to vary the rows according to the terrain of the site. While rows are not terraced on the hillside, as at Chatham Village, most of the buildings at Shalercrest are set into the slope such that their basement level is above ground on one side, providing space for additional apartment units and so greater variation in unit types.

In designing the row houses' interior plans, Stein worked to accommodate both traditional families and nontraditional households that might be necessitated by the war, such as groups of housemates or families taking in boarders. Some units provided an additional bathroom and double staircase, giving private access to each of two bedroom floors; others featured an extra bedroom that could be attached to one unit or the other.[22]

As Stein worked furiously toward a July 1, 1941, deadline for completing the designs of Stowe's Ohio View Acres and Shalercrest, he wrote of the breakneck pace to his wife:

Decisions must be made immediately. The work of the various technicians must be coordinated. The form of and plan of the house and the site work, the sewers, the water lines, the gas lines and the electric poles, the roads and paths and steps—every step just where it belongs and a place for the garbage can. And then the landscape work—each shrub and tree in its place, and each engineer must know what the other is doing so that the electric poles and the trees don't get in each other's way. They must know at once, so they waste no time, and we all finish on the dot.[23]

Stein had faced similar challenges at Chatham Village—how to comprehensively plan an efficient, affordable, yet comfortable residential community on a steeply sloping site—but now, ten years later, the circumstances were very different. His client, the Allegheny County Housing Authority, was a government bureaucracy, not a venturesome philanthropy; the existence of a conventional, winding suburban street constrained the possibilities of site design; and Stein had neither the luxury of time for in-depth preparatory studies nor the partnership of Henry Wright. As a site planner, Stein lacked Wright's genius, but his collaboration with Wright on the hillside site design of Chatham Village had been a formative experience, and at Shalercrest, Stein was able to apply many of their techniques sensitively, on a tight budget, and under pressure. He wrote to his friend Lewis Mumford in 1956, "I don't know if I told you that I did try my hand at developing hillsides, just outside of [Pittsburgh], some years after we did Chatham Village. . . . I think there is more to be learned from Chatham's 25 years of success."[24] As an architect and community designer, Stein continued to actively experiment with the vocabulary of the modern American garden city that he and Wright had established in the 1920s. While not as elegant as Chatham Village in terms of either architecture or site design, Shalercrest demonstrates that

Stein's approach to garden city–inspired residential planning was a dynamic one, open to expansion or contraction as circumstances demanded, and variable not only from site to site, but from client to client, budget to budget, and decade to decade.

Shalercrest was sold under a Mutual Home Ownership Plan in 1954 and reorganized as a for-profit corporation in 1980. Today, the community's housing association rents some units for income. Owners continue to hold shares in the community, and a mutual home ownership contract sets forth the responsibilities of the corporation to maintain building exteriors and systems, common areas, sidewalks, and trees, as well as those of the residents, who have free rein over their interior décor and the green spaces immediately outside their units. Although permission from the housing association board is required before residents may make changes, as at Aluminum City Terrace, the rules governing individual aesthetic expression have tended to foster more variety than consistency in Shalercrest's appearance. Formerly common courts along the pedestrian paths have been divided into individual yards and fenced with a variety of materials; the occasional garden shed serves as supplemental storage for residents living in small units with no attics, basements, or garages; original entrance canopies have been replaced or, in at least one case, enclosed to form a sun porch. At Shalercrest, the garden city vision of egalitarian architecture and communal open space has been superseded by individuals' desires to assert ownership over their own dwellings and yards.

Another defense housing project, while not attributed to Stein, bears a striking resemblance to his now-demolished Ohio View Acres in Stowe Township. Built by the federal government for shipbuilders and their families in 1943, Mooncrest is in Moon Township, adjacent to Stowe, fifteen miles northwest of Pittsburgh. Mooncrest is located high on a bluff overlooking the Ohio River and contains nearly four hundred townhouse units on 42.5 acres. Its street pattern is several loops accessed via a single connector, so that Mooncrest, while not laid out as a superblock, nevertheless functions as a self-contained enclave. Houses face onto, rather than away from, vehicular streets and are set back behind front yards as in a traditional suburb, but interior footpaths lead to neighborhood parks, and the scale of the community allowed Mooncrest to be built with its own school and grocery store (both long since closed). Buildings vary in length, but, as at Shalercrest, they are kept short in order to respond to the hilltop site. Mooncrest's greatest departure from the Chatham Village precedent is in its treatment of roads and automobiles. Though streets are integral to the design of and circulation within the community, there are neither garages, shared surface lots, nor alleys for the storage of vehicles. Today, residents tend to park their cars in cement pads poured on front lawns.

The units at Mooncrest were sold to their tenants in 1958, an ownership structure that has favored the community's preservation. As on Mt. Washington, residents tend to be long-term and committed, fostering a stable community of people who appreciate and maintain the unique characteristics of their surroundings. Unlike Chatham Village, Mooncrest has long been racially, economically, and generationally diverse.

Much as Charles Lewis deplored the idea of public housing, Chatham Village's influence on the national discourse on housing reform ultimately found expression there as well. In 1938, the year after the Wagner-Steagall bill established a national framework—and funding source—for public housing, the newly formed Housing Authority of the City of Pittsburgh initiated planning and construction of its first projects in the Hill District neighborhood, just east of downtown. Terrace Village and Bedford Dwellings were both developed on hilltop sites by a team that included Chatham Village architect William Boyd. Frederick Bigger was named chief consultant to the Housing Authority for the projects.

Figure 5.6. Terrace Village in the Hill District of Pittsburgh, 1951

Though the architectural team, and certainly Bigger, had Chatham Village in mind when designing for these two sites—both of which had topography that, like Mt. Washington, made the land inexpensive to acquire—these flagship public housing developments bore only a distant resemblance to the RPAA ideal. The first principle to be sacrificed was that of investment in quality. The United States Housing Act (USHA) of 1937 made federal funds available to local housing authorities, but limited costs per unit through required compliance with United States Housing Authority design stan-

Figure 5.7. Bedford Dwellings in the Hill District of Pittsburgh, 2009

dards. According to these standards federally funded low-income housing "will not be of elaborate or expensive design or material."[25] The low cost ceiling imposed by the USHA prohibited single-family or row housing as well as high-quality (and therefore high-cost) but low-maintenance materials and any aesthetic extras that might have enlivened the multifamily, "ribbon"-type apartment buildings that could be built within the budget.

This left architects such as William Boyd, whose predominant oeuvre was the so-called stockbroker Tudor, little option but to embrace the spartan Bauhaus aesthetic. When the federal government rejected the low bid for construction of Bedford Dwellings, the architects responded by eliminating a decorative strip of differently colored brick and entrance hoods on the exteriors of buildings, as well as tiled bathroom floors, cupboard doors, and numerous other small amenities on the interiors.[26] What was left was, arguably, barracks. At Terrace Village, too, the units were severely simple, inside and out. Recently, the buildings at Bedford Dwellings have been renovated; tellingly, among the domestic-scale amenities added to soften their severity and make them feel more like "home" were the entrance canopies that were cut from the design sixty years before.

The site planning of the projects did not redeem their architectural poverty. Thanks to Bigger's influence, undoubtedly, some glimmers of the Chatham Village idea shone through: two- and three-story apartment buildings faced interior courts that featured walkways, drying yards, playgrounds, tenant gardens, and, at Bedford Dwellings, a community building and pool. At Terrace Village, the layout even featured curvilinear streets and cul-de-sacs. But the rigid geometry of the flat-roofed, ribbon-style buildings, whether arrayed severely in rows as at Bedford Dwellings or on a meandering street plan as at Terrace Village, resisted the kind of imaginative response to the contours of the land that characterized Chatham Village.

In the botched translation of the eloquent Chatham Village idea to an "economical" plan for housing the city's poorest citizens, worst of all were the unintended consequences of the superblock. On Mt. Washington, the superblock's tendency to foster an isolated enclave served merely to cocoon a middle-class community. At the public housing complexes, superblocks gave stark physical definition to patterns of socioeconomic segregation, creating islands of poverty with all its attendant ills within the project's borders and stigmatizing its residents from without.

Even Catherine Bauer, who had been at the forefront of the push for public housing in the 1930s, admitted as early as 1957 that, unlike social security, public housing had not "become accepted as an integral part of the normal scheme of things," due in part to the physical design of the projects themselves.[27]

Ravaged by crime and deterioration and largely abandoned by the 1990s, Terrace Village today is gone. It has been replaced by Oak Hill, a neo-traditional community featuring a mix of incomes, housing designs, and materials on a more conventional grid street plan.

Beyond those communities planned in direct imitation of Chatham Village, it has been said that "Every architect, engineer or land planner who ever laid out a cul de sac, designed a superblock, built green areas around houses or apartments, faced living rooms to rear gardens or planned safety streets for children owes a debt" to the designers of the Pittsburgh neighborhood.[28] On one hand, this can be seen as a tribute to the enduring genius of Chatham Village and its planners. Scholar Eugenie Birch has noted that while suburban Planned Unit Developments (PUDs) represent the most minimal application of garden city planning, they do demonstrate the tenacity and marketability of garden city principles.[29] On the other hand, this observation speaks to the diffusion, debasement even, of the Chatham Village idea, the components of which were often applied a la carte rather than comprehensively and in coordination with one another as the original planners intended. Chatham Village's imitators might utilize a superblock site to achieve grouped dwellings, communal open space, and separation of automobile and pedestrian circulation, but these factors alone do not guarantee the richly rewarding environment that Stein and Wright achieved on Mt. Washington.

The designers of Chatham Village achieved harmony and restrained complexity through what Clarence Stein called "the rational relationship of the individual parts"—a reciprocal combination of architecture, planning, and site design. Stein explained, "every detail down to the last house and the view from the windows must be conceived, planned, and built as a related part of a great setting for . . . living and working."[30] In Stein and Wright's scheme, houses are clearly related to one another and to the landscape. The architecture is uniform, simple, and relatively—but not entirely—unadorned. It is also egalitarian. There is variety, but no one building asserts itself as more important than the others. Materials, consistent throughout Chatham Village, are of such inherent quality that they need not be disguised: red brick, slate, limestone, wood, and iron. Relief from monotony comes from subtle variations of detail, such as roof shape or cornice treatment, and the stepped and terraced rhythms of the rows of houses as they ride the rugged terrain and enclose landscaped courtyards, no two of which are alike. The greenbelt effectively insulates the community from outside noise, traffic, and social factors.

Few who attempted to follow the Chatham Village model achieved this level of subtlety and complexity. Some did not have enough—space, money, time, talent—to work with. Others failed because they applied the Chatham Village idea piecemeal: a courtyard here, a row of brick houses there. But this was like baking with only part of the recipe. Without the chemistry of all the ingredients combined in their proper proportions, the results were bland and flat.

Other developments modeled on Chatham Village made the mistake of substituting "cheap" for "economical." The Buhl Foundation's demonstration was, after all, justly famed for its efficient and affordable construction; later imitations by lesser designers offered affordability at the expense of quality—of materials, of architecture, of site design. This became especially true as Modernism began to eclipse eclecticism as the dominant architectural mode in the late 1930s and early 1940s. The "honest" Bauhaus aesthetic, in which form followed function, became, in many cases, a convenient ex-

Figure 5.8. Ornamental details are simple and consistent throughout Chatham Village.

cuse for paring house design down to its most miserly basics. This, in turn, was most apparent where budgets were most constrained: in the public housing projects designed after Chatham Village in the late 1930s. Small wonder that these projects built on the cheap have proven expensive over the years, whether measured by the social pathologies their environments fostered or by the demolition and/or radical reconstruction that have been necessary to keep these projects functioning. While Chatham Village has thrived with nothing more than modest, regular maintenance, its publicly built successors quickly fell into disrepair, disrepute, and, ultimately, disuse.

The importance of site design is another critical lesson of Chatham Village. Imitators often employed a rigid geometry to their site planning that implies domination over, rather than response to, their sites. Today, in an era when site preparation often means little more than using bulldozers and retaining walls to create level lots for building more of "the same," the planning of Henry Wright shows how design that works with, not against, a challenging site can lower costs while increasing attractiveness and marketability. Residents themselves respond to Chatham Village's site-inspired design: the buildings' interaction with a dynamic topography augments the simplicity of the architecture, creating a whole greater than the sum of its parts.

The dumbing-down of the Chatham Village idea into a set of stock concepts in subdivision design made it less compelling, while the failure of public housing and garden-variety garden apartment communities to achieve the success of Chatham Village led to doubts about, and finally the discrediting of, superblock-style planning. Commitment to building large-scale planned communities of the type advocated by Lewis, Bigger, Stein, and Wright ultimately diminished into halfhearted efforts to weave neighborhood unit principles into the planned tract layouts of Levittowns and suburban PUDs. True planned communities in the mode of Chatham

Figure 5.9. Chatham Village architects specified high-quality, durable materials, such as wrought iron for porch supports, to minimize long-term costs of repair and replacement.

Village were more frequently built abroad, most notably in Scandinavia and Britain, than at home.

Ada Louise Huxtable, longtime architecture critic for the *New York Times*, offered an additional explanation for why Chatham Village, successful as it was, did not inspire more development in its image. She notes that Stein, Wright, and the RPAA endorsed a kind of sensitive, humane, idealistic planning that was part of the culture of the 1920s and 1930s, when the answer to many of the ills of society seemed to be, simply, a better place to live. In later decades, "this ideal was exploded by racial tensions and by the discovery that social malaise lies in the bedrock of complex human problems and deep-rooted inequities to which better physical planning offers few, if any, answers. And some of its most basic and widely used principles—the public ownership of land, for example, to avoid speculative exploitation and to provide the service infrastructure and community facilities that require long-term, up-front investment—are still generally unacceptable in the United States." Because of the inadequacy of this kind of commitment, Huxtable asserts, the Johnson administration's New Town experiments of the 1960s were successful in and of themselves, but suffered Chatham Village's earlier fate of becoming much-admired islands in the midst of conventionally developed tracts. The planning principles of Chatham Village represent a "rational, compassionate, idealistic, and somewhat simplistic and naïve philosophy," yet, "it worked for the middle class, [and] it is not without relevance now."[31]

Perhaps the history of Chatham Village proves that there can be no perfect community in an imperfect world. Yet the Buhl Foundation's experiment is truly not without relevance now. It was, after all, a successful demonstration that an investment in quality of planning, design, and construction pays reliable limited dividends to its builder—and exceedingly handsome ones to its residents.

six Preservation and Planning for a New Urbanism

Chatham Village did not have to revolutionize American housing in order to set a powerful example. In the words of Clarence Stein, a planned community "leaves a record of human ideals and purposes that may last beyond its time."[1] Beyond its purpose as a Depression-era housing demonstration, Chatham Village—along with other planned communities— has much to teach us about the application of planning theories to the realities of city life. Taken together, planned communities embody the experiments we have tried and the lessons we have learned about building better places to live, all of which inform our activities today as we plan for the future.

For this reason, the preservation of historic planned communities is a critical concern. The preservation of Chatham Village, in particular, is relevant not only to its own future, but to the futures of many other early twentieth-century planned communities, including others designed by Stein and Wright and those developed with Chatham Village as a prototype. These communities are the manifestations, in space and matter, of an important phase in the history of ideal models for (largely) middle-class ways of life, a phase that has had a vast, if fractured, influence on all subsequent large-scale development in the United States. The ways these places were built tell us much about how architects and planners once thought we should live. The ways they were used tell us much about how they did or did not succeed—valuable lessons for contemporary planners concerned with the same issues of efficient, affordable, walkable, green development.

The stability and struggles of Chatham Village and other early twentieth-century planned communities reveal the limitations of planning for an ideal society. The history of planned communities is the history of ideals of social as well as physical order; like many planned communities, Chatham Village represents the ideas of one group of people about how another group should live. Yet, like architectural styles, social norms and aspirations are constantly revised, and, like any communities, planned ones must adapt to changing times. To a historian, a planned community's lack of integrity—representing areas where the planning did not address the reality or the reality did not stay the same—may be as fascinating as its sameness over time.

Chatham Village today is a National Historic Landmark, a designation reserved for those places which have made the most profound and lasting impacts on American history. But the Buhl Foundation's demonstration in housing is no fossil; it is a living, thriving community three-quarters of a century after it was built. Ardently maintained and protected by a dedicated community of residents, Chatham Village was planned for lasting vitality and value.

Built to inspire a revolution in housing, Chatham Village has never known revolution from within. This scrupulously planned environment was not built to grow and change, except under the explicit direction and close supervision of its creators; one might even say it was planned for preservation, not just of its physical fabric, but of a way of life. Despite fundamental changes in its ownership and management, not to mention larger patterns and practices of urbanism, Chatham Village continues to look and operate much as it did in the 1930s.

Preservation in a planned community poses different challenges than in a conventional historic district. More than a group of buildings, a planned community is a marriage of idea and reality; it is a blueprint for a way of life as well as a place in which to live it. To date, the preservation profession has not produced any guidelines for the preservation of planned communities, but observation of Chatham Village and its "sister" RPAA communities suggests that such guidelines should address three major principles. We might call these the ideal community, the whole community, and the real community.

The "ideal community" refers to the fact that planned communities, almost without exception, embody social ideals in their designs for physical spaces. Some are social or religious utopias built to isolate residents from an outside world they do not favor. Others, like Chatham Village, are didactic demonstrations, while still others are less ambitious attempts to improve upon existing patterns of development, or to foster some social commodity—for instance, safety, homogeneity, or community—that appears to be threatened in contemporary urban or suburban life. All have at their core a mode of living, interacting, and often working that their creators considered ideal. This vision is expressed in both physical and social constructions that seek to guide, improve, and regulate the community residents' lives.

At Chatham Village, the ideal community is expressed in the density and privacy simultaneously afforded by single-family row houses; in these houses' orientation toward common interior courtyards; in the egalitarianism of the architecture; in the reuse of the Bigham mansion as a community clubhouse; and in the Village's landscape amenities, designed to bring city dwellers into daily contact with nature and, in the case of the greenbelt, provide a physical and social buffer between Chatham Village and the surrounding community.

The "whole community" refers to the fact that planned communities are built, often (though not by any means always) all at one time, according to a unifying principle of design. The buildings of Chatham Village, for instance, were constructed in three phases, but an essential design vocabulary was repeated throughout each one to promote a feeling of unity.[2] In a planned community even more than in a speculatively developed one, the architecture of an individual building often cannot be evaluated solely on its own merits, but must be viewed in the context of the integrity of the whole. Buildings, landscape, site plan, transportation routes, and other deliberate aspects of the planned community are all integral, interdependent elements, and their significance rests on being understood as such.

The "real" community refers to the way these rigorously planned environments are experienced and used by their residents after they are built. Social ideals may prove faddish, flawed, or ultimately untenable when built in bricks and mortar; they are rarely maintained for as long as the communities themselves. In addition, since historic planned communities are often the result of one group of people's ideas about how a certain, not necessarily similar, stratum of society should live, they may be condescending at worst and, at best, naïve.

Figure 6.1. The Village Green, formerly known as Baldwin Hills Village, in Los Angeles has become condominiums.

The real community tends to coexist within the whole and ideal communities, creating varying degrees of tension among them. Chatham Village stands in marked contrast to contemporary projects by the same designers, but whose physical integrity has been compromised over the years by residents who either could not or did not choose to live within the original community's plan. Sunnyside Gardens, where residents divided their communal courtyards into small, fenced, private backyards as soon as their restrictive covenants expired, is an extreme example of the real community asserting itself over the whole and ideal communities as planned by Stein and Wright. At Baldwin Hills Village, a later project designed by Stein in Los Angeles, the central "Village Green" has been transformed into a putting green, and children are no longer welcome on the interior courtyards and walks.

Figure 6.2. Built as large-scale, affordable rental housing, Buckingham Village in Arlington, Virginia (shown here in 1937), has not been maintained as such.

Buckingham, Virginia, the first major community designed in Chatham Village's image and with a site plan by Henry Wright, has been fractured by the tensions inherent in preserving a community of historically affordable rental units in a heated real estate market. Part of Buckingham has been listed on the National Register of Historic Places and maintained as affordable rentals. But another section has been converted to condominiums, and over three hundred original units have been demolished so that the land can be redeveloped as luxury townhomes and high-rises.

At Radburn, residents more subtly revised the intended program for use of their carefully planned neighborhood. Alden Christie, an architecture student and Radburn resident, offered the following observations about that community in 1964:

Neighboring Radburn cul-de-sacs have no social connection. Interests are turned inward. The kitchen becomes the inelegant focal point for all outside activity, which consists of "across the pavement" contacts. . . . The children play more in the lanes than in the parks. . . . The layout of the dwellings in the superblocks creates a network of intensely developed spaces which abruptly evaporate into a shapeless common, too vaguely defined to suggest an extension or expansion of private yards, too wide to command a directional tendency towards a focal point, too sparsely landscaped to invite a refuge from the tight complex of houses . . . the automobile has been made such a dominant feature of the Radburn scheme that life is more oriented towards the peripheral access road . . . than towards the common green.[3]

In Christie's observations, the whole community—the physical representation of the ideal—is incoherent and inconsistent with actual patterns of human behavior, and he identifies the ways in which the real community compensates for this. Of course, Christie's comments may be taken either as criticisms of the planning and design concepts that informed Radburn or as evidence of their adaptability.[4]

These experiences tell us that, while the origins of a planned community are important, its physical design represents a particular moment in time that is continually reevaluated by subsequent generations. To understand a planned community, we must understand the evolving meaning of the physical environment to a changing society of residents.

Aside from the mature landscape, Chatham Village betrays little evidence of time's passage for three reasons: a policy of common exterior maintenance, resulting in consistent exterior repair since the beginning; the prohibition of individual expression on the exteriors of houses; and the concealment of technology. Cars are still relegated to perimeter roads and tucked-away garages; utilities are still buried underground. When television came to Chatham Village, a master antenna was installed for the community as a whole so that rooftops would not bristle with individual antennas throughout. Chatham Village remains, as its architects hoped it would be, an aesthetic refuge from the world of the machine, even while it is built to be served by them. It also remains a community that is cared for and about by its residents. Its well-maintained, well-regulated appearance is the product of consistent management and maintenance, unified ownership, and respect for community values.

Chatham Village is, above all, a stable community. Preservation is a compatible value there because, fundamentally, this community has never been about change. From the subtle evocations of colonial heritage in its architecture to its deliberate exclusion of destabilizing elements and technological trappings, Chatham Village has always been about staying the same.

In large part, this is because Chatham Village's developers did their homework, devoting two years to exhaustive research and study before the first brick was laid. Its designers were experts who had tried their hand on previous projects and learned from their own successes and mistakes. Chatham Village is not a collection of generic design gimmicks like so many "planned" suburbs today, but benefits from a city-, neighborhood-, and site-specific plan. Because the special requirements of the both the land and its residents were understood and accommodated, the community's physical and social planning have tended to serve them both well.

In developing a long-term investment, the Buhl Foundation saw the value of construction that, while initially more expensive, would require minimal outlay for maintenance down the road. Chatham Village was built to last. Moreover, from 1932 to 1960 the foundation, under the consistent and watchful leadership of Charles Lewis, guarded the design integrity of the community. Since the conversion to cooperative ownership, the house committee of the corporation has functioned much as a local historic preservation commission to ensure the continued integrity of the Chatham Village aesthetic. It sets guidelines for what types of individual expres-

Figure 6.3. Consistent policies regarding exterior maintenance and repair have resulted in a unified appearance of all the Chatham Village homes from 1932 to the present.

sion are and are not permissible on homes. In addition, it conducts design review over all exterior and interior alterations. Sanctions for violation include fines and, in extreme cases of refusal to comply, eviction. Permitted additions include awnings, as long as they are of green canvas;[5] patios; and exterior storm windows. Exterior additions that are expressly prohibited include carports or porches and porticoes of any kind (except as part of approved patios), and the enlargement of any unit beyond its existing exterior envelope. Political signs may not be displayed in windows, and exterior repainting is allowed only in the original colors: cream for wooden window sash and deep emerald green for doors and ironwork on balconies and porches. On the interior, only the addition of extra bedrooms is expressly disallowed.

Stored in the basement of the Chatham Manor apartment building are original fixtures—wooden doors, fireplace mantels, stair handrails and spindles, porcelain pedestal sinks, toilets, tubs, radiators, lighting fixtures, and more—that have been removed during remodeling projects during the past several years. Rather than allow these to be discarded, Chatham Village Homes, Inc. has retained them so that any member who might wish to restore an interior space to its original appearance may do so with the original furnishings. In addition, original blueprints of all the units and various historic photographs and other materials are available for the perusal of members curious about their unit's original design or the community's history.

Individual residents of Chatham Village may or may not describe themselves as preservationists, but they have an abiding respect for community values, which is the foundation of the preservationist's ethic. After all, one of preservation's fundamental assumptions is that the physical artifacts of the past nourish our common historical awareness. Residents of Chatham Village are comfortable with the idea of the common good; their community itself is founded upon this principle.

That there is a strong foundation for a preservation ethic

among the residents of Chatham Village is, of course, no accident. There is a reciprocal relationship between the concept of the planned community and its preservation. In a way, residents of Chatham Village are self-selected to care about the perpetuation of their community's historically significant features. With its uniform design, modest row houses, and minimal private property, Chatham Village appeals to those who place the restrained beauty of the entire community above the all-American values of robust individual expression. Once they move into such a community, these people are generally supportive of efforts to protect it. Those unwilling to live within the house committee's strict guidelines do not make it through the membership screening process.

As we have seen, the long-term maintenance of the entire property has done much to perpetuate the coherent character of the community. Whether tenants or shareholders, the residents have never been allowed to perform exterior alterations on their homes. Instead, responsibility for exterior maintenance has been centralized in the management office since its opening in 1932, and thus has remained consistent. This approach to maintenance at Chatham Village has, over the years, served to preserve its characteristic harmony of design.

The combined effects of these measures have been to keep the meticulously planned and designed environment of Chatham Village very much intact. Some small changes, such as enlarged garages to accommodate the oversized cars of the 1960s and 1970s, have occurred, and because the resident population today is demographically different from that for whom the Village was built, the environment is differently used. The sandboxes and safe play spaces for children, for instance, are often empty. Because of the prevalence of working adults, including more professional women than stay-at-home mothers, the members' rules and regulations specify times when certain noisy toys may not be used and prescribe the number of children allowed to play together in the courtyards (more than three must take their games elsewhere). There are still ample times and places for children to play games as well as roller skate, skateboard, and ride bicycles in Chatham Village, but the emphasis seems to have shifted from a nurturing environment for families with small children to one which emphasizes the needs of adults.

Returning to Chatham Village some fifty years after its construction, its landscape architect, Ralph Griswold, remarked: "It's wonderful that [Chatham Village] could hold its identity. It hasn't changed in character one particle. The plants are bigger and fuller, but the people, the use, the appearance is identical. . . . In this country, land changes hands so often, and new guys come in with new ideas. Chatham Village has survived [intact], and it's a wonder."[6]

Of all the history lessons of Chatham Village, perhaps the most striking is that its planners set out to address the very same set of issues urban planners wrestle with today. In the 1920s and 1930s, Lewis, Bigger, Stein, and Wright looked around at the dominant mode of residential development and saw a dysfunctional wasteland of uninspired, resource-intensive, overpriced housing that did not respond to the human needs of its residents for community with one another and with nature. They saw the automobile and its demands for space and services beginning to dominate the form and scale of neighborhoods, towns, and cities.

In response, these progressive planners strove to provide affordable housing; an alternative to public housing; a sustainable, walkable, livable community; a transit-oriented development; and a green community that incorporated both nature and new technology into modern patterns of work and recreation. They aspired to develop an alternative to suburban sprawl and its waste of scarce resources. As early as the 1930s, Henry Wright called for "a less wasteful and more effective pattern" than that of conventional speculative real estate development, "a fairly compact and carefully related community organization rather than the loosely organized sprawling suburban expansion of the last few decades."[7] Wright and his contemporaries were, in other words, prescient in their understanding of the urban condition of the twentieth, and even the twenty-first, century.

But unlike twenty-first-century planners, Chatham Village's planners assumed they would have to pioneer a new urban form—to break utterly with the past to achieve their goals. Clarence Stein wrote passionately of "how unworkable and wasteful are the obsolete patterns of old cities, and how completely they demand replacement. It is futile to attempt this in a small, piecemeal manner."[8] Stein believed the nineteenth-century city had become archaic, while Wright, laying groundwork for the urban renewal policies of thirty years hence, came to advocate the wholesale clearance and rebuilding of blighted urban areas. Theirs was a cataclysmic vision of a broken urban form that must be eradicated to make way for a new, modern paradigm for living. Today, we can see this in perspective. Contemporary planners, in particular the New Urbanists, have emerged from a half-century of experimentation with systematically destroying and drastically rebuilding the city to circle back to the seemingly simple, timeless, functional model of the traditional urban form: the dense, walkable, mixed-used grid.

The New Urbanism, a community-building and design movement primarily founded by planners Andres Duany and Elizabeth Plater-Zyberk in the 1980s, today advocates the preservation of old neighborhoods and the design of new ones with such traditional features as a regular street grid to provide flexible, permeable, easily navigable circulation; a legible center to act as a community focal point; sidewalks to promote walkability; alleys to direct vehicles to come and go by the rear; small lots to allow for density; front porches to encourage community; a mix of housing types to invite diversity; and the use of regional building styles and materials to promote a sense of place.[9]

Since its emergence as a distinct movement, complete with a charter and a professional, promotional organization—the Congress for the New Urbanism—in the early 1990s, the

New Urbanism has proved wildly popular among not only urban thinkers and theorists but among the rank and file of homebuyers and renters who are, after all, the city's true constituents. Also, whereas the first New Urbanist communities, such as Seaside, Florida, and Kentlands, Maryland, were actually self-contained suburbs built on greenfields outside of cities,[10] in more recent years New Urbanism has become increasingly urban. Its tenets have informed infill projects, both residential and commercial, within city limits. Prominent examples in Pittsburgh include Washington's Landing, in which an upscale community of houses, offices, and recreational amenities was built on an island formerly degraded by decades of toxic uses; Summerset at Frick Park, in which a neighborhood of homes, neo-traditional on the outside but thoroughly modern in floor plans and amenities within, were constructed on a former slag heap adjacent to a major city park; and South Side Works, in which a mixed-use residential/retail development has been more or less successfully knitted into an adjacent historic district.

In addition, many of Pittsburgh's distressed public housing projects, most notably Terrace Village, have been the beneficiaries of government HOPE VI grants to transform them into New Urbanist–style neighborhoods characterized by mixed-income residency, individual dwelling units (as opposed to large, shared apartment buildings), and defensible space, bearing out the idea that safety and security can be enhanced by appropriate environmental design. HOPE VI, a program of the Department of Housing and Urban Development, has distributed billions of dollars through Community Development Block Grants since 1992 to reconfigure public housing nationwide from dysfunctional "projects"—frequently characterized by austere apartment buildings set within minimally landscaped superblocks, as exemplified by Bedford Dwellings—to low-rise, pedestrian-friendly communities with individual front doors, front porches, and improved connections to their surrounding communities.

Figure 6.4. Summerset at Frick Park in Pittsburgh

Figure 6.5. South Side Works in Pittsburgh

While Stein, Wright, and their colleagues considered the grid pattern of urban streets deeply flawed, even deadly, and streets themselves an unconscionably wasteful form of open space, the New Urbanism approaches the street grid as fundamental and highly functional shared public space, defined by the architecture that frames it. In New Urbanist developments, as in traditional neighborhoods, sidewalks follow the street; homes front onto it and face one another across it. Windows and the semipublic spaces of porches enhance safety by providing "eyes on the street." Streets intersect to form blocks and blocks add up to form neighborhoods—an infinitely replicable urban network, unlike the superblock, which eventually must have an edge, whether buffered by a greenbelt or, more frequently, forming an abrupt boundary between planned community within and traditional city or suburb without.

New Urbanist neighborhoods take varying approaches to the car. Some include alleys, removing garages and much vehicular access from building frontages and segregating (in theory if not always in practice) comings and goings of vehicles to the rear of properties, leaving pedestrian-scale features such as paths, porches, and doorways to dominate facades. In New Urbanist communities without garages, street parking may be viewed as a safety buffer between the pedestrian on the sidewalk and the active automobile on the street, and parking lots are frequently found on the interiors of blocks, where the planners of the 1930s concentrated pedestrian amenities such as walking paths and landscaped courtyards. In a reversal of the superblock paradigm, the New Urbanists value street frontages as the face of the community, and view the real estate on the interiors of blocks as more suitable for vehicle storage since it is hidden from the street. Sidewalks, which follow the street grid, provide pedestrians with access to an infinite network of routes and destinations, unlike interior pathways, which direct circulation within a neighborhood without reference to the city without.

Figure 6.6. Pedestrian path in the early Chatham Village

Figure 6.7. At Chatham Village today, cars are still relegated to perimeter roads and the interior is accessible only to pedestrians.

When it was first developed and demonstrated, the planning paradigm of Stein, Wright, and their contemporaries was the New Urbanism of its day. And it was, truly, new: the communities they planned represented a complete break from what they viewed as an obsolete urban form and a more satisfying alternative to the cookie-cutter suburbia even then burgeoning on the city's edge. In designing their inwardly focused New Towns, however, these planners underestimated the importance of integration into the broader urban context. In encouraging architecture that was egalitarian, they discouraged a diversity of households and incomes within their carefully calibrated enclaves. And the planning ideals of the RPAA were seldom achieved, even by its members, let alone by imitators. The best examples of New Town planning, such as Chatham Village, are today verdant oases glimmering amid repetitive tracts of conventional development. The worst have become known, simply, as "the projects."

Today's New Urbanism also has its critics, who decry it as being, variously, nostalgic, retrograde, elitist, and no more sustainable than the sprawl it purports to address. Yet our culture's overwhelming embrace of the New Urbanism has led to a widespread reappraisal of traditional urban forms at a time when cities themselves, a generation ago all but abandoned by the middle class, are undergoing a dramatic reversal of fortune. Crime is down, fuel costs are up, and cities, far from being broken, are enjoying a renaissance as the creative nerve centers of our new knowledge-based economy.

In rearticulating the neighborhood as the all-important building block for communities, the New Urbanism has revived perhaps the most important tenet of the 1930s New Town planners. Equally significant, the New Urbanism has revived a Baroque emphasis on the formal public realm—as distinct from informal public spaces—in its approach to building successful, satisfying new communities. This was an element missing from New Town planning, which assumed that shared social and economic activity would be enough to create community identity.[11]

The resurgence of the traditional—and neo-traditional—city has also contributed to the discrediting of the superblock and other innovations of the large-scale planning of the 1920s and 1930s. This style of neighborhood planning has become stigmatized through association with the mean public housing projects and harshly inhumane urban renewal plans that emerged after Chatham Village in the mid-twentieth century. Meanwhile, the "old" urbanism rejected so resoundingly by Clarence Stein and Henry Wright has stood the test of time. It has reemerged from fifty years of assault—including by the RPAA's vision of the American garden city—to be reappraised as the most viable, flexible, functional, and replicable model for the human living environment.

Yet in terms of creating places where there is some *there* there, the RPAA's vision, as exemplified by Chatham Village, is still a compelling model with much to teach us about the integration of human needs—for a well-designed, well-built environment, for nature in the city, for options in transportation, for each other—into a compact urban form that is designed to conserve land, resources, and money. Chatham Village was built to work and built to last. It was, after all, a sustainable community before the phrase was coined.

Meanwhile, the New Urbanism is just that: new. Its long-term success has not been proven. It is tempting to predict success based on the persistence of its time-tested model, but we should keep in mind that traditional cities and towns, whether old or new, are fallible, too. In an article on nostalgia and the New Urbanism, A. Joan Saab points out that the movement's emphasis on the "re" (as in reintegration, revitalization) "presumes the existence of an integrated and vital community life in the past. In many instances, however, New Urbanist plans overlook the flaws within the traditions that they are evoking."[12]

Like a New Town, a New Urbanist community can be well planned and soundly built, or it can end up as a pastiche of superficially, haphazardly, or cheaply applied gimmicks. As Chatham Village has developed a patina of well-maintained maturity, so are the best New Urbanist communities likely to have enduring value. Others, less well planned and built, may fare little better in several decades than banal post–Chatham Village garden apartment complexes. Time will tell.

This is not to set up a false dichotomy between the New Urbanism and the New Town planning that created Chatham Village. Indeed, the New Urbanism is descended from the American New Town tradition, itself an adaptation of Ebenezer Howard's garden city formula. New Urbanism thus emerges from a long history of utopian town-planning ideals that seek to link aesthetics, politics, and everyday life by redesigning the human habitat.[13] Although Howard was reacting to the overcrowded urban squalor of industrial London, Stein and Wright to the dangerous and congested urban grid,[14] and the New Urbanists to the physical sprawl and social anomie of twentieth-century American suburbia, the movements share a bedrock assumption: that a deliberately designed built environment can foster vitality in civic life.

New Town planning and the New Urbanism also hold in common core community values. The goal of the Congress for the New Urbanism to "reintegrate the components of modern life—housing, workplace, shopping and recreation—into compact, pedestrian-friendly, mixed-use neighborhoods linked by transit and set in a larger regional open-space framework,"[15] could have been lifted directly from an RPAA manifesto. This hints at the fact that, like the RPAA's New Towns, the New Urbanism is not particularly urban. Both movements share, as their primary concern, an aspiration to reshape the sprawling "middle ground" of automobile-oriented suburbia between existing dense urban centers and the open, rural countryside, which, by virtue of better suburban planning, will stand a greater chance of being preserved.

To this end, both New Towns and New Urbanism depend on certain specific traits. Both promote an interconnected but variable street pattern; a system of public parks and open spaces; a hierarchy of streets designed with shade trees and sidewalks; a walkable town or neighborhood center; a separation of industrial, but not commercial, uses from residential ones; and attention to local context, particularly as expressed in building materials and historic architectural styles.[16] Above all, New Towns and New Urbanism hold one fundamental principle in common: the value of the neighborhood, defined as a legible residential area anchored by businesses and institutions that serve the immediate community.

New Town planning and the New Urbanism, then, share a set of fundamental assumptions and goals about the importance of the scale and design of the built environment in shaping meaningful, sustainable communities. They part

Figure 6.8. A view of the pedestrian-oriented interior of Chatham Village, 1936

ways on the best paths to realizing them. In an ideal world, even more ideal, perhaps, than that envisioned by Charles Lewis and his cohort of progressive community planners, both visions would coexist as viable options for building and rebuilding the neighborhoods of our future. In any case, we would do well not to rely exclusively on any one formula for urban revitalization. Cities are complex organisms whose vitality depends on the presence and balance of a great many factors including, but not limited to, the placement of buildings, sidewalks, and streets. Any theory of urbanism, new or old, can influence some of these factors, but can truly succeed only where everything—physical, social, economic—comes together. Community planning, wrote Clarence Stein, "starts not with aesthetic conception but with exploration, unveiling, discovery."[17] If the history of planning in the twentieth century has taught us anything, it is the importance of this. We have seen all too tragically the failure of a doctrinaire approach. Planning has proven to be a very particular practice. Small interventions can have profound consequences. Massive ones more often devastate than rejuvenate.

By the same token, there is a coherence to any great vision that is essential to its realization, and so we must also resist the temptation to treat any planning model as a collection of stock concepts to be mined for "best practices." No demonstration of community planning, no matter how persuasive, can be taken apart and applied piecemeal and succeed. Just as a New Town superblock can create a coherent enclave or a dysfunctional ghetto, just as a row of houses can be a delightful complexity or a monotonous barrack, the keys to New Urbanist development take their meaning from their whole contexts. A front porch or a clock in a brick-paved square may be a symbol of community or an empty gesture, depending on its relationship to the environment around it.

Ultimately, no community, and no theory for community-building, has it all. People make and demand choices. They may want to safari in the concrete jungle by day, but retreat to a leafy cul-de-sac by night. They may want to walk to work and have a mother-in-law flat over their two-car garage. They may want to raise their children among a diversity of neighbors, or they may want to live in a place that caters to people very much like themselves. Urbanism, be it new or old, succeeds when it creates special places where people want to live, work, and socialize. Beyond this, it is not doctrinaire about its form.

In understanding Chatham Village's broad significance despite its limited influence, we should look not only at its failures, but at one of the paradoxical secrets of its success:

Figure 6.9. Chatham Village, 1934

Chatham Village was, and is, not for everyone. One of the reasons it works so well is that it remains a unique choice in the Pittsburgh housing market, and the people who choose to live there value what Lewis, Stein, and Wright created. It's an insular, middle-class, park-like, attractive, safe environment, highly regulated and closely guarded by its residents and owners. It exists within the old city, and alongside the new, as a model for extraordinarily well-planned and, yes, sustainable development that continues to be viable long after its initial influence has faded.

At the end of *Toward New Towns for America*, Clarence Stein wrote, "When an idea becomes conventional, it is time to think it through again. Never-ending exploration and the charting of new ways is the life force of the architect and the New Town planner, whose shield of battle should bear the simple device—the question mark."[18]

Stein himself resisted the idea that Chatham Village, or any of the New Town communities he designed in his lifetime, represented a full solution to the problems of cities or suburbs. "Each [of the communities]," he wrote, "is limited but rich in suggestions. . . . They are living experiences, not blue prints."[19] As a living experience, Chatham Village has stood the test of time; its balance of vitality and stability is a testament to the power of planning to create a community of enduring value, from the Great Depression into the twenty-first century. In the search for a truly sustainable community, we would do well not to leave the demonstration of Chatham Village in the past, but to carry it forward into the future.

Notes

Chapter 1: The Architects of a Solution

1. The national housing crisis during and after World War I is discussed in Roy Lubove, *Community Planning in the 1920s: The Contribution of the Regional Planning Association of America* (Pittsburgh: University of Pittsburgh Press, 1963), 17–22.

2. Roy Lubove, *Twentieth-Century Pittsburgh*, vol. 1, *Government, Business, and Environmental Change* (New York: John Wiley and Sons, Inc., 1969; Pittsburgh: University of Pittsburgh Press, 1995), 63. Citations refer to the 1995 edition.

3. Lubove, *Community Planning*, 19–21.

4. President Hoover is quoted in Lewis Mumford, "The Planned Community," *Architectural Forum* 58, no. 4 (Apr. 1933): 253.

5. Lewis Mumford to Roy Lubove, quoted in Lubove, *Community Planning*, 40.

6. Lemuel Shattuck, *Report of the Sanitary Commission of Massachusetts, 1850* (Cambridge, MA, 1948), 208, quoted in Lubove, *Community Planning*, 70.

7. Lubove, *Community Planning*, 70–71.

8. Donald Lisio, "Investing in Pittsburgh's Progress: The History of the Buhl Foundation" (PhD diss., University of Wisconsin, 1964), 57, 58.

9. Lisio, "Investing," 54.

10. Lewis Mumford, "A Modest Man's Enduring Contributions to Urban and Regional Planning," *AIA Journal* (Dec. 1976): 20, 22.

11. Kermit C. Parsons, "Clarence Stein and the Greenbelt Towns: Settling for Less," *American Planning Association Journal* 56, no. 2 (Spring 1990): 165.

12. Mumford, "Modest," 19.

13. Parsons, "Clarence Stein," 165.

14. Parsons, "Clarence Stein," 165.

15. Mumford, "Modest," 19.

16. Clarence Stein, *Toward New Towns for America* (Cambridge, MA: MIT Press, 1951; rev. ed., 1957), 219. All subsequent citations refer to the revised edition.

17. Mumford, "Modest," 20.

18. Cynthia L. Girling and Kenneth I. Helphand, *Yard Street Park: The Design of Suburban Open Space* (New York: John Wiley and Sons, Inc., 1994), 54.

19. Parsons, "Clarence Stein," 166.

20. Philip D'Anieri, "A 'Fruitful Hypothesis'? The Regional Planning Association of America's Hopes for Technology," *Journal of Planning History* 1, no. 4 (Nov. 2002): 281–84.

21. Carl Sussman, ed., *Planning the Fourth Migration: The Neglected Vision of the Regional Planning Association of America* (Cambridge, MA: MIT

Press, 1976), 22–23, quoted in John F. Bauman and Edward K. Muller, "The Planning Technician as Urban Visionary: Frederick Bigger and American Planning, 1913–1954," *Planning History Studies* 10, nos. 1–2 (1996): 29.

22. Kristin Larsen, "Cities to Come: Clarence Stein's Postwar Regionalism," *Journal of Planning History* 4, no. 1 (Feb. 2005), 36.

23. D'Anieri, "'Fruitful Hypothesis,'" 286.

24. Lubove, *Community Planning*, 126.

25. Mumford, "Modest," 24; Parsons, "Clarence Stein," 171–72.

26. Mumford, "Modest," 26.

27. Ada Louise Huxtable, "Clarence Stein: Forgotten Prophet," in *Architecture, Anyone?* (New York: Random House, 1986), 36.

28. Perhaps because his career was cut short by an untimely death or because he left few personal papers behind, Wright remains a neglected figure in urban planning history. Historians have tended to view him in the shadow of Stein, although Stein himself viewed their partnership as one of equals. The best sources of information on Wright's life and career are those that deal with Stein and the RPAA, obituaries of Wright (cited in this work), and Wright's projects, articles, and book, *Rehousing Urban America* (New York: Columbia University Press, 1935).

29. Clarence Stein, "Henry Wright: 1878–1936," *American Architect and Architecture*, Aug. 1936, 23.

30. Wright, *Rehousing Urban America*, preface.

31. Stein, "Henry Wright," 24.

32. Henry Wright, "Hillside Group Housing," *Architectural Record* 72, no. 2 (Oct. 1932): 221–31.

33. Wright, "Hillside Group Housing," 221–31.

34. Richard Pommer, "The Architecture of Urban Housing in the United States During the Early 1930s," *Journal of the Society of Architectural Historians* 37, no. 4 (Dec. 1978): 262.

35. Clarence Stein to Aline Stein, Jul. 1, 1933. Clarence Stein Papers and Letters, 3600, Cornell University Archives.

36. Eric Mumford, "The 'Tower in the Park' in America: Theory and Practice, 1920–1960," *Planning Perspectives* 10, no. 1 (1995): 21–22.

37. Pommer, "Architecture," 262.

38. Lubove, *Community Planning*, 40.

39. This argument is presented by John F. Bauman and Edward K. Muller in "Planning Technician," 22. Bauman and Muller, also the authors of *Before Renaissance: Planning in Pittsburgh 1889–1943* (Pittsburgh: University of Pittsburgh Press, 2006) are the only writers to focus on Bigger's considerable role in urban planning history. Though, as they point out, he practiced planning for half a century, held important and influential public offices, associated closely with many of the profession's greatest luminaries and was involved in some of the nation's most important planning events, Bigger left few personal papers or other biographical aids when he died, and he has been virtually ignored by planning historians.

40. William H. Wilson, *The City Beautiful Movement* (Baltimore: Johns Hopkins Press, 1989), quoted in Bauman and Muller, "Planning Technician," 23.

41. Frederick Bigger, "Pittsburgh and the Pittsburgh Plan," *Art and Archaeology* 14 (1922): 269–77, quoted in Bauman and Muller, "Planning Technician," 26.

42. Bauman and Muller, "Planning Technician," 32.

43. Suburban Resettlement Administration, *Statement of General Policies and Objectives of the Suburban Resettlement Administration*, Oct. 1, 1935, John S. Lansill Papers, University of Kentucky Libraries, quoted in Bauman and Muller, "Planning Technician," 32.

44. Bauman and Muller, "Planning Technician," 33.

45. Bauman and Muller, "Planning Technician," 33, 34, 31.

Chapter 2: Precedent and Process

1. Stephen V. Ward, "Ebenezer Howard: His Life and Times," in *From Garden City to Green City*, ed. Kermit C. Parsons and David Schuyler (Baltimore: Johns Hopkins University Press, 2002), 18.

2. Ebenezer Howard, *Garden Cities of To-morrow* (Cambridge, MA: MIT Press, 1965), 10.

3. Girling and Helphand, *Yard Street Park,* 55.

4. Johnston Birchall, "Co-Partnership Housing and the Garden City Movement," *Planning Perspectives* 10, no. 4 (1995): 333.

5. Edith Elmer Wood, *Recent Trends in American Housing* (New York: Macmillan, 1931), 11, quoted in Gail Radford, *Modern Housing for America: Policy Struggles in the New Deal Era* (Chicago: University of Chicago Press, 1996), 31.

6. Catherine Bauer, *Modern Housing* (Boston: Houghton Mifflin, 1934), plate 45.

7. Stein, *Toward New Towns,* 44.

8. National Park Service, "Roland Park Historic District," *Baltimore: A National Register of Historic Places Travel Itinerary* (Washington, D.C.: National Park Service, 2002).

9. Susan L. Klaus, *A Modern Arcadia: Frederick Law Olmsted, Jr., and the Plan for Forest Hills Gardens* (Boston: University of Massachusetts Press, 2002), 4.

10. Bradley D. Cross, "'On a Business Basis': An American Garden City," *Planning Perspectives* 19, no. 1 (2004): 66.

11. Edith Elmer Wood, *Inhabited Alleyways in the District of Columbia,* 63rd Congress, 2nd session, May 7, 1914, 24, 25, quoted in Radford, *Modern Housing for America,* 36.

12. Radford, *Modern Housing for America,* 38.

13. Alexander von Hoffman, "The End of the Dream: The Political Struggle of America's Public Housers," *Journal of Planning History* 4, no. 3 (Aug. 2005): 236.

14. Raymond Unwin, *Town Planning in Practice: An Introduction to the Art of Designing Cities and Suburbs* (1909; reprint, London, T. F. Unwin, 1920), 164, quoted in Lubove, *Community Planning,* 49–50.

15. Andrew J. Thomas, the New York architect responsible for the Metropolitan Life Insurance apartments in Queens, represented an important early-1920s effort to achieve economies and improvements in design and site planning through the use of the city block as the basic building unit, reduced land coverage, compactness in design, grouping of open spaces into courts and gardens, and intensive cost analysis. Roy Lubove wrote that Thomas provided a link between Unwin's ideas and the work of Stein and Wright at Sunnyside and Radburn. See Lubove, *Community Planning,* 503–4, and Richard Plunz, *A History of Housing in New York* (New York: Columbia University Press, 1990), chap. 5, especially pp. 135–37.

16. Clarence Stein, "Housing and the Depression," *Octagon,* June 1933, 4.

17. Stein, "Housing and the Depression," 4.

18. Stein, "Housing and the Depression," 4.

19. Mumford, "Planned Community," 253.

20. Stein, "Housing and the Depression," 5.

21. Stein, *Toward New Towns,* 22, 47, 37.

22. Stein, *Toward New Towns,* 41.

23. Stein, *Toward New Towns,* 47.

24. Mervyn Miller, "Garden Cities and Suburbs: At Home and Abroad," *Journal of Planning History* 1, no. 1 (Feb. 2002): 18.

25. Geddes Smith, "A Town for the Motor Age," *Survey Graphic,* 1930, quoted in Stein, *Toward New Towns,* 44.

26. Girling and Helphand, *Yard Street Park,* 60.

27. Charles F. Lewis, "Limited Dividend Housing: To the Board of Managers, June 5, 1930," Buhl Foundation Archives, Historical Society of Western Pennsylvania, 6, 9.

28. Lewis, "Limited Dividend Housing," 19, 18.

29. Charles Lewis, "The Housing Situation," *Pittsburgh Sun,* Dec. 21, 1926, 6.

30. Clarence S. Stein and Henry Wright, "Preliminary Report of Clarence S. Stein and Henry Wright," Dec. 29, 1930, Buhl Foundation Archives, Historical Society of Western Pennsylvania, 1.

31. Wright, *Rehousing Urban America,* 50.

32. The Bigham estate has an interesting history of its own. Consisting of wooded hills, rugged cliffs, and rolling table land, the seven-hundred-acre tract was part of a proprietary grant to William Penn from King Charles II in the year 1681. In 1768, Penn's heirs confirmed the title by purchasing the land from the Iroquois Indians. After the American Revolution, it became part

of the "Manor of Pittsburgh," one of several large tracts that were allowed by the new Commonwealth of Pennsylvania to remain in the possession of the Penn heirs after the revoking of the Proprietary Charter.

In 1794 the tract was purchased by Major Abraham Kirkpatrick, who had come to Pittsburgh in 1767, fought for Virginia in the Revolution, and returned to Pittsburgh after peace had been re-established. Major Kirkpatrick died in 1817, leaving three daughters (the major's only son died at the age of 20). One daughter married Dr. Joel Lewis, a soldier and physician; another married Christopher Cowan, an early ironmaster; and the third married the Hon. Charles Shaler, lawyer and jurist. Upon Major Kirkpatrick's death, the land was divided into three sections, with the Shalers taking the western, the Cowans the eastern, and the Lewises the central portion. The daughter of Dr. Lewis, Maria Louisa, married lawyer and publisher Thomas J. Bigham, who built Bigham Hall on his wife's property. Their son, Kirk Q. Bigham, and daughter, Mary (Mrs. Melville M. Stout), continued to own and occupy the parcel known as the Bigham estate until they sold it to the Buhl Foundation in 1931, at which point they moved into a new home nearby on Bigham Street (C. V. Starrett, "Old Bigham House has Romantic History," *Chatham Village News*, Dec. 1932, reprinted in *Chatham Village News*, Fiftieth Anniversary Edition, Oct. 10, 1982).

33. "A Brief History of Mt. Washington," *Mt. Washington News*, June 3, 1976, 3.

34. Ralph Griswold, "Wright Was Wrong," *Landscape Architecture* 53 (Apr. 1963): 209.

35. Charles Lewis, "Pittsburgh Housing Inquiry," Oct. 6, 1930, Buhl Foundation Archives, Historical Society of Western Pennsylvania, 2.

36. Frederick Bigger, "Report of Frederick Bigger: A Development for the Bigham Tract, Mt. Washington," Oct. 15, 1930, Buhl Foundation Archives, Historical Society of Western Pennsylvania, 4.

37. Bigger, "Report of Frederick Bigger," 7, 6.

38. Stein and Wright, "Preliminary Report of Stein and Wright," 2.

39. Stein and Wright, "Preliminary Report of Stein and Wright," 2.

40. Stein, *Toward New Towns*, 76.

41. Lewis, "Limited Dividend Housing," 10.

42. Bigger, "Report of Frederick Bigger," 7.

43. Herbert Emmerich, "Report on Pittsburgh Housing Situation," Nov. 17, 1930, Buhl Foundation Archives, Historical Society of Western Pennsylvania, 6.

44. The Buhl Foundation, "Report for the Years 1929–1930," Buhl Foundation Archives, Historical Society of Western Pennsylvania, 34, quoted in Lisio, "Investing," 223–24.

45. Emmerich, "Report on Pittsburgh," 6.

46. Charles Lewis, "A Moderate Rental Housing Project in Pittsburgh," *Architectural Record* 70, no. 4 (Oct. 1931): 217–34.

47. Wright, *Rehousing Urban America*, 50.

48. Charles Lewis, "Buhl Foundation Report," June 30, 1955, reprinted in *Chatham Village News*, Fiftieth Anniversary Edition, Oct. 10, 1982, 2.

49. Lisio, "Investing," 228.

50. Stein, *Toward New Towns*, 85.

51. Edith B. Wallace and Paula S. Reed, with Linda McClelland, "Chatham Village National Historic Landmark Nomination," 2003, 24.

52. Lisio, "Investing," 232–34.

53. Stein, *Toward New Towns*, 85.

54. Wright, *Rehousing Urban America*, 50.

55. Stein, *Toward New Towns*, 85.

56. Wright, *Rehousing Urban America*, 50.

Chapter 3: Design for a Modern Village

1. Wright, *Rehousing Urban America*, 36.

2. Lewis believed that housing was the "orphan" of business, neglected by respected business leaders, and therefore dominated by greedy speculators concerned solely with profits. He thought the most effective long-term solution was the consolidation of the housing industry into a tightly organized, powerful national corporation such as General Motors, which would be able to lower building costs by controlling quarries, brickyards, forests, lumber mills, and factories. Charles

Lewis, "Housing—The Orphan on the Doorstep," *Pittsburgh Record*, Oct.-Nov. 1931, 24, quoted in Lubove, *Twentieth-Century Pittsburgh*; see also Lisio, "Investing," 229.

3. The Buhl Foundation, "Study of Names for Housing Project," Oct. 23, 1931, Buhl Foundation Archives, Historical Society of Western Pennsylvania.

4. In her book *Building the Dream: A Social History of Housing in America* (Cambridge, MA: MIT Press, 1981), Gwendolyn Wright notes that the quaint early American period styles that characterized suburban architecture in the 1920s and early 1930s suggested deep racial and ethnic insecurities, even hostilities, among established ethnic-majority Americans. Wright points out that the popularity of these architectural styles correlates with a period of backlash after the country's greatest wave of immigration during the years around the turn of the century. In the 1920s, laws were passed placing quotas on immigration, and some ethnic groups were barred from entering the United States altogether. Wright says that architectural styles such as Chatham Village's Georgian Revival "provided acceptable cultural references" for white families "trying to establish their heritage and their place in the world" (210–11).

5. Stein said, "Chatham Village is one of the outstanding American examples of housing and site planning. I feel free to say this because the site plan was mainly the work of my associate Henry Wright. He had a feeling for the shape of the ground and what could be done to mold it to the practical needs of home and community that seemed superhuman" (*Toward New Towns*, 76).

6. Stein, *Toward New Towns*, 41.

7. Stein, *Toward New Towns*, 78.

8. Frederick Bigger, "More Limited Dividend Housing: The Buhl Foundation Project in Pittsburgh," *Octagon* 3 (Oct. 1931): 7.

9. William Boyd, "What Period Our Homes? Practical Needs, Not Convention, Governed Design," *Chatham Village News*, Oct. 19, 1932, 3.

10. Boyd, "What Period," 3.

11. Charles T. Ingham, "Village Architect Compares Modern, 'Chatham' Styles," *Chatham Village News*, Mar. 1, 1934, 2.

12. Ingham, "Village Architect," 2.

13. Charles Lewis, "Chatham Village Extension: Some Considerations for Discussion," Mar. 29, 1935, Buhl Foundation Archives, Historical Society of Western Pennsylvania, 6.

14. Lewis, "Chatham Village Extension," 6.

15. Lewis, "Chatham Village Extension," 8.

16. Lewis, "Chatham Village Extension," 10.

17. "Limited Dividends Pay," *Architectural Forum* 65 (Aug. 1936): 159.

18. Each house retains a small patch of garden (between its front door and the walkway), which may be planted with flowers. Vegetable gardens are prohibited except in community garden patches set aside for that purpose near the tennis courts. Chatham Village, "Rules and Regulations," author's collection, Sept. 1990.

19. Later, Griswold received international acclaim for his designs for Pittsburgh's Point State Park and for restoring the Agora, the marketplace at the base of the Acropolis in Athens.

20. Ralph E. Griswold, "Preliminary Report on Landscape Development for Mt. Washington Housing Development," c. Oct. 1931, Buhl Foundation Archives, Historical Society of Western Pennsylvania, 1.

21. Griswold, "Preliminary Report," 2.

22. Griswold, "Preliminary Report," 3.

23. Griswold, "Preliminary Report," 3.

24. For the woodland landscape plan, see Charles Lewis and Theodore M. Kohankie, "Chatham Village Woodland Development," June 18, 1937, Buhl Foundation Archives, Historical Society of Western Pennsylvania.

25. Charles Lewis, "Chatham Village: Apartment, Garages, Workrooms," Apr. 15, 1955, Buhl Foundation Archives, Historical Society of Western Pennsylvania, d.

26. Stein, *Toward New Towns,* 85.

27. Lewis, "Chatham Village: Apartment, Garages, Workrooms," d–f.

28. Lewis, "Chatham Village: Apartment, Garages, Workrooms," d–f.

29. During much of the first half of the twentieth century, film decency codes required that twin beds be depicted in married couples' sleeping quarters. Gwendolyn Wright notes that the influence of the movies was such that twin beds became a fad among real married couples. See Wright, *Building the Dream*, 209–10.

30. Lewis, "Buhl Foundation Report," 2.

31. Lewis, "Chatham Village," h.

Chapter 4: The Social Life of a Planned Community

1. Rose C. Weibel, "Social and Housing Conditions in the Bigham District, Mt. Washington," Apr. 21, 1931, Buhl Foundation Archives, Historical Society of Western Pennsylvania, 7.

2. Weibel, "Social and Housing," 5.

3. Charles Lewis to Buhl Foundation managers, cover letter to Weibel, "Social and Housing Conditions."

4. David Vater, a longtime resident of Chatham Village and student of its history, speculates that the Buhl Foundation specifically selected people from outside of the existing Mt. Washington community in order to ensure that residents would develop ties to one another and that a coherent Chatham Village community would form. Though undocumented, he infers this rationale from the fact that none of the early Chatham Village residents were from the Mt. Washington neighborhood (David Vater, personal communication with author, Oct. 1997 and Jul. 1998). The same theory is suggested in "An Idea— and an Ideal," written in 1938 by an anonymous original resident of Chatham Village who observed: "The fact that most residents came to the Village from distant parts of the city had much to do with developing a higher degree of self-sufficiency than exists in most neighborhoods" ("An Idea—and an Ideal," 1938, printed in the *Chatham Village Times* 6, no. 3, Mar. 1998, 3–8).

5. "An Idea," 6.

6. Weibel, "Social and Housing," 3.

7. Lisio, "Investing," 248.

8. Emmerich, "Report on Pittsburgh," 6.

9. Quoted in Lewis, "Buhl Foundation Report."

10. Charles Lewis, "Housing: A Program for Administration," Nov. 18, 1931, Buhl Foundation Archives, Historical Society of Western Pennsylvania, 3.

11. Lewis, "Housing: A Program," 3.

12. *Chatham Village News* 14, June 11, 1945.

13. Lewis, "Housing: A Program," 6.

14. "An Idea," 5.

15. The Chatham Village tenant selection criteria are not made explicit anywhere in the extant Buhl Foundation records. Perhaps they were literally unwritten rules, or perhaps they were destroyed before the foundation's papers were donated to a public archive. This description of the early deliberate demographics at Chatham Village is based on interviews with longtime residents Albert Vestal, Mary Williams, and David Vater, conducted by the author in July 1998.

16. Lubove, *Twentieth-Century Pittsburgh*, 81.

17. "Partnership" was the word used by Lewis to describe the reciprocal commitment of tenants and management needed to ensure Chatham Village's success. Essentially, the foundation's financial investment in planning and construction would be matched by the tenants' emotional investment in maintaining the social stability of their surroundings. See Lewis, "Housing: A Program," 6.

18. Lewis, "Housing: A Program," 6.

19. Lewis, "Housing: A Program," 6, 7, 4.

20. Lisio, "Investing," 239.

21. Lewis, "Housing: A Program," 6.

22. Lewis, "Housing: A Program," 8.

23. To write this section, the author relied on oral histories and interviews supplied by longtime Chatham Village residents Albert Vestal, Gene Gundrum, and Mary Williams in interviews conducted in July 1998, as well as "An Idea."

24. "An Idea," 3.

25. "An Idea," 3.

26. David Vater, "Chatham Village Historic District." National Register of Historic Places Registration Form, Oct. 1990.

27. Charles Nutting, quoted in David Bollinger, "Chatham Village Sale in Works," *Pittsburgh Press*, Dec. 30, 1959, 4.

28. "Village Here Being Sold in Co-op Deal," *Mt. Washington News*, Jan. 8, 1960, 1, 8; "Chatham Village Gets Blueprint for Co-op," *Mt. Washington News*, Feb. 5, 1960, 1.

29. Kathryn Nelson, former manager of Chatham Village Homes, Inc., interview with author, Jul. 24, 1998.

30. David Bollinger, "Chatham Village Gets Lowdown," *Pittsburgh Press*, Jan. 29, 1960, 20.

31. Jane Jacobs, *The Death and Life of Great American Cities* (New York: Random House, 1961), 64.

32. These demographic trends occur despite the best efforts of the cooperative board's membership committee, which attempts to achieve an age balance in the community "in sync with society" at large. See Bill Steig, "Housing Project, 30s Gem, Thrives Quietly Amid City," *Pittsburgh Post-Gazette*, Jul. 26, 1980, 15.

33. "Chatham Village Revisited," *Architectural Forum* 112 (May 1960): 120.

34. Steig, "Housing Project, 30s Gem," 15.

35. David Vater, interview with author, Oct. 1997.

36. Bigger, "Report of Frederick Bigger," 7.

37. Birchall, "Co-Partnership Housing," 336–54.

38. Residents note that even into the 1970s, after the corporation ceased discriminating on grounds of race, class, and religion, it continued to exert some control over the demographics in the community, striving for a balance of ages.

Chapter 5: A Demonstration, Not a Revolution

1. Lewis, "Buhl Foundation Report," 2.

2. Bauer, *Modern Housing*, 239.

3. Lisio, "Investing," 227.

4. Wallace and Reed, "Chatham Village," 24–25.

5. Wallace and Reed, "Chatham Village," 26.

6. Oscar Fisher, "Buckingham: Housing Laboratory," *Architectural Record* 83 (Jan. 1938): 69–82.

7. Charles F. Lewis, interview with Donald Lisio, Aug. 31, 1961, quoted in Lisio, "Investing," 263.

8. "Housing Plan Seen as a 'Walled City,'" *New York Times*, May 20, 1943, 23.

9. Clarence S. Stein, "Investment Housing Pays," *Survey Graphic*, Feb. 1940, 77.

10. Currently under the ownership of a realty company, Hancock Village is the subject of a controversial proposal to expand its housing offerings. See John Hilliard, "Developer: Hancock Village Expansion Will Move Ahead," *Wicked Local Brookline*, Aug. 10, 2010. See also "Brookline Faces Decision on Huge Housing Proposal," *Christian Science Monitor*, Jan. 5. 1946, 5; Massachusetts Historical Commission, "Hancock Village," Historic Resource Inventory Form A, May 2008, Massachusetts Archives Building, Boston.

11. Lisio, "Investing," 260.

12. Clarence Stein to Aline Stein, Nov. 28, 1936, in Kermit Parsons, ed., *The Writings of Clarence S. Stein: Architect of the Planned Community*, Baltimore: Johns Hopkins University Press, 1998, 369.

13. "Large-Scale Housing: Its Past, Its New Status . . . Its Problems . . . Its Possibilities," *Architectural Forum*, Feb. 1938, 113, 110.

14. Michael H. Lang, "Town Planning and Radicalism in the Progressive Era: The Legacy of F. L. Ackerman," *Planning Perspectives* 16 (2001): 155.

15. Lubove, *Twentieth-Century Pittsburgh*, 82.

16. Lisio, "Investing," 273.

17. Kristin M. Szylvian, "Bauhaus on Trial: Aluminum City Terrace and Federal Defense Housing Policy During World War II." *Planning Perspectives* 9, no. 3 (1994): 236.

18. Kristin Szylvian Bailey, "Defense Housing in Greater Pittsburgh: 1945-1955," *Pittsburgh History*, Spring 1990, 20.

19. Szylvian, "Bauhaus on Trial," 236–42.

20. Szylvian Bailey, "Defense Housing," 18.

21. Clarence Stein to Aline Stein, June 26, 1941, in Parsons, *Writings of Clarence S. Stein*, 420.

22. "Low-Cost Houses," *Architectural Forum*, Oct. 1941, 233.

23. Clarence Stein to Aline Stein, June 26, 1941, in Parsons, *Writings of Clarence S. Stein,* 420.

24. Clarence Stein to Lewis Mumford, Jul. 29, 1956, in Parsons, *Writings of Clarence S. Stein,* 571.

25. John F. Bauman, "The History and Significance of Housing Authority of Pittsburgh Projects: PA-1-2 and PA-1-8 (Bedford Dwellings and Bedford Dwellings Addition): PA-1-3 (Allequippa Terrace); and PA-1-6 (Broadhead Manor)." Prepared for the Housing Authority of the City of Pittsburgh, Development and Modernization Division, 1997, 9. On the relationship of the federal standards to the standards developed by Henry Wright, see E. Mumford, "Tower in a Park," 25.

26. Bauman, "History," 10.

27. Catherine Bauer, "The Dreary Deadlock of Public Housing," *Architectural Forum* 106 (May 1947): 140–221.

28. "Clarence Stein: Land Planning's Man of Influence," *House and Home,* May 1956, 169.

29. Eugenie Birch, "Five Generations of the Garden City: Tracing Howard's Legacy in Twentieth-Century Residential Planning," *From Garden City to Green City: The Legacy of Ebenezer Howard,* ed. Kermit C. Parsons and David Schuyler (Baltimore: Johns Hopkins University Press, 2002), 181.

30. Stein, *Toward New Towns,* 225.

31. Huxtable, "Clarence Stein: Forgotten Prophet," 38.

Chapter 6: Preservation and Planning for a New Urbanism

1. Stein, *Toward New Towns,* 226.

2. Vater, "Chatham Village Historic District," sect. 7.

3. Alden Christie, "Radburn Reconsidered," *Connection* 7, May 25, 1964, 37–41, quoted in Girling and Helphand, *Yard Street Park,* 66.

4. Girling and Helphand, *Yard Street Park,* 66.

5. These have a historical precedent, having appeared on Chatham Village homes in early photographs.

6. Steig, "Housing Project, 30s Gem," 15.

7. Wright, *Rehousing Urban America,* preface.

8. Stein, *Toward New Towns,* 218.

9. The guiding principles of the New Urbanism are set forth in several sources that informed this work, including: Congress for the New Urbanism, *Charter of the New Urbanism* (New York: McGraw-Hill, 2000); Peter Katz, *The New Urbanism: Toward an Architecture of Community,* (New York: McGraw-Hill, 1994); Peter Calthorpe, *Ecology, Community, and the American Dream* (Princeton: Princeton Architectural Press, 1993); and Andres Duany and Elizabeth Plater-Zyberk, *Towns and Town-Making Principles,* ed. Alex Krieger with William Lennertz (New York: Rizzoli, 1991).

10. Vincent Scully dubbed the movement the New Suburbanism. See Scully, afterword to Katz, *New Urbanism,* 221.

11. William Fulton, "The Garden Suburb and the New Urbanism," in Parsons and Schuyler, *From Garden City to Green City,* 169.

12. A. Joan Saab, "Historical Amnesia: New Urbanism and the City of Tomorrow," *Journal of Planning History* 6, no. 3 (Aug. 2007), 192.

13. Saab, "Historical Amnesia," 195.

14. Fulton, "Garden Suburb," 163.

15. "New Urban Communities," www.newurban communities.com, quoted in Saab, "Historical Amnesia," 192.

16. This list is adapted from one in Suzanne Sutro Rhees, "From Riverside to Seaside: Historic Planned Communities, 1880s–1990," paper presented at the Seventh National Conference on American Planning History, Seattle, Oct. 23. 1997, quoted in Fulton, "Garden Suburb," 161.

17. Stein, *Toward New Towns,* 226.

18. Stein, *Toward New Towns,* 227.

19. Stein, *Toward New Towns,* 217.

Bibliography

"AIA Gold Medal for Clarence Stein Salutes Planning Attuned to People." *Architectural Forum* 104 (May 1956): 21.

Arlington Heritage Alliance. *Arlington Heritage Alliance Releases Sixth Annual 'Arlington's Most Endangered Places' List.* June 7, 2006.

Bauer, Catherine. "The Dreary Deadlock of Public Housing," *Architectural Forum* 106 (May 1957): 140–221.

———. *Modern Housing.* Boston: Houghton Mifflin, 1934.

Bauman, John F. "The History and Significance of Housing Authority of Pittsburgh Projects: PA-1-2 and PA-1-8 (Bedford Dwellings and Bedford Dwellings Addition); PA-1-3 (Allequippa Terrace); and PA-1-6 (Broadhead Manor)." Prepared for the Housing Authority of the City of Pittsburgh, Development and Modernization Division, Feb. 1997.

Bauman, John F., and Edward K. Muller. *Before Renaissance: Planning in Pittsburgh, 1889–1943.* Pittsburgh: University of Pittsburgh Press, 2006.

———. "The Planning Technician as Urban Visionary: Frederick Bigger and American Planning, 1913–1954." *Planning History Studies* 10, no. 1–2 (1994): 21–39.

Bigger, Frederick. "More Limited Dividend Housing: The Buhl Foundation Project in Pittsburgh." *Octagon* 3 (Oct. 1931): 3–7.

Birch, Eugenie. "Radburn and the American Planning Movement: The Persistence of an Idea." *Journal of the American Planning Association* 46, no. 4 (Oct. 1980): 424–39.

Birchall, Johnston. "Co-Partnership Housing and the Garden City Movement." *Planning Perspectives* 10, no. 4 (1995): 329–55.

Bollinger, David. "Chatham Village Co-op Deal Closed." *Pittsburgh Press*, June 8, 1960.

———. "Chatham Village Gets Lowdown." *Pittsburgh Press*, Jan. 29, 1960, 20.

———. "Chatham Village Goes Co-op in History-Making Transaction. *Pittsburgh Press,* Nov. 16, 1960, 37.

———. "Chatham Village Sale in Works." *Pittsburgh Press*, Dec. 30, 1959, 4.

Boyd, William. "What Period Our Homes? Practical Needs, Not Convention, Governed Design." *Chatham Village News*, Oct. 19, 1932, 3.

"A Brief History of Mt. Washington," *Mt. Washington News*, June 3, 1976, 3.

"Brookline Faces Decision on Huge Housing Proposal," *Christian Science Monitor*, Jan. 5. 1946, 5.

Buhl Foundation Archives. Historical Society of Western Pennsylvania, Pittsburgh.

Calthorpe, Peter. *Ecology, Community, and the American Dream.* Princeton: Princeton Architectural Press, 1993.

Chase, Stewart. "The Case Against Home Ownership." *Survey Graphic* 27 (May 1938): 261–67.

"Chatham Manor Opens in Famous Village." *Pittsburgh Post-Gazette*, Feb. 25, 1956.

"Chatham Seeks Fair Market Value." *Pittsburgh Press*, Apr. 12, 1985.

"Chatham Village Gets Blueprint for Co-op." *Mount Washington News*, Feb. 5, 1960, 1.

Chatham Village Homes, Inc. "Articles of Incorporation." Author's collection, June 15, 1960.

———. "Buyer's Guide." Author's collection, c. 1997.

———. "By-Laws." Author's collection, undated.

———. "Chatham Village." Marketing brochure. Author's collection, c. 1995.

———. "Chatham Village: A Timeless Community." Marketing brochure. Author's collection, 1976.

———. "Occupancy Agreement." Author's collection, 1998.

———. "Rules and Regulations." Author's collection, Sept. 1990.

Chatham Village House Committee. "Standard Text for Renovation Approvals." Author's collection, Jul. 1990.

"Chatham Village Revisited." *Architectural Forum* 112 (May 1960): 118–21.

"Chatham Village Sale on Boards." *Pittsburgh Post-Gazette*, Dec. 31, 1959.

"Chatham Village, Second Unit, Pittsburgh, Pennsylvania." *Architecture* 150 (Feb. 1937): 63–66.

"Civilized Living, Chatham Village." *Housing*, Nov. 1934.

"Clarence Stein Remembered." *AIA Journal* 65 (Dec. 1976).

"Clarence Stein: Land Planning's Man of Influence." *House and Home* (May 1956): 169–73.

Comey, Arthur C., and Max S. Wehrly. "Chatham Village, Pittsburgh, PA." *Planned Communities* 2 (1939).

Congress for the New Urbanism. *Charter of the New Urbanism.* New York: McGraw-Hill, 1994.

Cotton, Anne Boyer. "Clarence S. Stein and His Commitment to Beauty: Architecture First, Community Planner Second." Master's thesis, Cornell University, 1987.

Courtsal, Francis Chase. "The Incomparable Chatham Village." *Pennsylvania Illustrated*, Apr. 1978.

Creese, Walter L., ed. *The Legacy of Raymond Unwin: A Human Pattern for Planning.* Cambridge, MA: MIT Press, 1967.

Cross, Bradley D. "'On a Business Basis: An American Garden City." *Planning Perspectives* 19, no. 1 (2004): 58–77.

D'Anieri, Philip. "A 'Fruitful Hypothesis'? The Regional Planning Association's Hopes for Technology." *Journal of Planning History* 1, no. 4 (Nov. 2002): 279–89.

"Dr. Lewis Steps Down at Buhl Foundation." *Pittsburgh Press*, Jul. 22, 1956.

Duany, Andres, and Elizabeth Plater-Zyberk. *Towns and Town-Making Principles.* New York: Rizzoli, 1991.

Estrada, Louis. "Buckingham: Change and Diversity." *Washington Post*, Nov. 19, 1994.

Fisher, Oscar. "Buckingham: Housing Laboratory." *Architectural Record* 83 (Jan. 1938): 69–82.

Fuller, Martin. "Planning for a Better World: The Lasting Legacy of Clarence Stein." *Architectural Record* 170, no. 10 (Aug. 1982): 122–27.

Gangewere, R. Jay. "Henry Buhl, Jr. and 'The Everlasting Getting On With It.'" *Carnegie Magazine* 59 (Nov.–Dec. 1989): 4, 32–35.

Garwood, Bret Conover. "Clarence S. Stein and Hillside Homes: Precedents for Planning Low Income Housing and Designing Community Architecture in New York City." Master's thesis, Cornell University, 1998.

Girling, Cynthia L., and Kenneth I. Helphand. *Yard Street Park: The Design of Suburban Open Space.* New York: John Wiley and Sons, Inc., 1994.

Griswold, Ralph E. "Wright Was Wrong." *Landscape Architecture* 53 (Apr. 1963): 209–14.

Hancock, John Lorentz. "John Nolen and the American City Planning Movement: A History of Culture Change and Community Response, 1900–1940." PhD dissertation, University of Pennsylvania, 1964.

Hardy, Dennis. "Garden Cities: Practical Concept, Elusive Reality." *Journal of Planning History* (Nov. 2005): 383–91.

Hilliard, John. "Developer: Hancock Village Expansion Will Move Ahead." *Wicked Local Brookline*, Aug. 10, 2010.

"Housing Group to Fight Sale of Six Projects." *Pittsburgh Press,* Feb. 7, 1953.

"Housing Plan Seen as a 'Walled City.'" *New York Times*, May 20, 1943, 23.

Howard, Ebenezer. *Garden Cities of To-morrow.* 1898. Reprinted Cambridge, MA: MIT Press, 1965.

Howard, H. H. "Large-Scale Housing Difficult to Finance." *Pittsburgh Sun-Telegraph*, Mar. 3, 1937.

Huxtable, Ada Louise. "Clarence Stein: The Champion of the Neighborhood." *New York Times*, Jan. 16, 1977.

———. "Clarence Stein: Forgotten Prophet." In *Architecture, Anyone?* New York: Random House, 1986.

"An Idea—and an Ideal," unpublished anonymous

essay, 1938, published in *Chatham Village Times* 6, no. 3 (Mar. 1998).

Ingham, Charles T. "Village Architect Compares Modern, 'Chatham' Styles," *Chatham Village News*, Mar. 1, 1934, 2.

"Institute's Gold Medal for 1956." *AIA Journal* 25, May 1956.

Jacobs, Jane. *The Death and Life of Great American Cities*. New York: Random House, 1961.

Katz, Peter. *The New Urbanism: Toward an Architecture of Community*. New York: McGraw-Hill, 1994.

Klaus, Susan L. *A Modern Arcadia: Frederick Law Olmstead, Jr. and the Plan for Forest Hills Gardens*. Amherst: University of Massachusetts Press, 2002.

Lang, Michael H. "Town Planning and Radicalism in the Progressive Era: The Legacy of F. L. Ackerman." *Planning Perspectives* 16, no. 1 (2001): 145–67.

"Large-Scale Housing: Its Past, Its New Status . . . Its Problems . . . Its Possibilities." *Architectural Forum*, Feb. 1938, 110–24.

Larsen, Kristin. "Cities to Come: Clarence Stein's Postwar Regionalism." *Journal of Planning History* 4, no. 1 (Feb. 2005): 33–51.

Lewis, Charles F. "The Buhl Foundation Builds a Second Unit of Chatham Village," *American City* 50 (Sept. 1935): 81–82.

———. "Buhl Foundation Report," June 30, 1955. Reprinted in *Chatham Village News*, Fiftieth Anniversary Edition, Oct. 10, 1982, 2.

———. "Chatham Village: A Study in Planning." *Real Estate Record*, May 16, 1936.

———. "Community Housing in Pittsburgh." *City Planning* 7, no. 4 (Oct. 1931): 260–61.

———. "Foundation to Make Housing Demonstration." *American City* 45 (Jul. 1931): 115.

———. "The Housing Situation," *Pittsburgh Sun*, Dec. 21, 1926, 6.

———. "An Investment Approach to the Housing Problem." *Real Estate Record*, Mar. 20, 1937.

———. "A Moderate Rental Housing Project in Pittsburgh." *Architectural Record* 70, (Oct. 1931): 217–34.

"Limited Dividend Roll Call," *Architectural Forum* 62 (Jan. 1935): 98–103.

"Limited Dividends Pay." *Architectural Forum* 65 (Aug. 1936): 159–60.

Lisio, Donald. "Investing in Pittsburgh's Progress:

The History of the Buhl Foundation." PhD diss., University of Wisconsin, 1964.

"Low-Cost Houses," *Architectural Forum*, Oct. 1941, 233.

Lubove, Roy. *Community Planning in the 1920s: The Contributions of the Regional Planning Association of America*. Pittsburgh: University of Pittsburgh Press, 1963.

———. *Twentieth-Century Pittsburgh*. Vol. 1, *Government, Business, and Environmental Change*. New York: John Wiley and Sons, 1969. Reprinted Pittsburgh: University of Pittsburgh Press, 1995. Page references are to the 1995 edition.

MacFayden, Dugald. *Sir Ebenezer Howard and the Town Planning Movement*. Manchester: Manchester University Press, 1933.

Marx, Leo. *The Machine in the Garden*. London: Oxford University Press, 1964.

Massachusetts Historical Commission. "Hancock Village." Historic Resource Inventory Form A, May 2008. Massachusetts Archives Building, Boston.

Mayer, Albert. "Henry Wright: Creative Planner." *Survey Graphic* 25, no. 9 (Sept. 1936): 530.

McKenzie, Evan. *Privatopia: Homeowner Associations and the Rise of Residential Private Government*. New Haven: Yale University Press, 1994.

Miller, Donald. "Village on the Mount." *Pittsburgh Post-Gazette*, May 17, 1990.

Miller, Mervyn. "Garden Cities and Suburbs: At Home and Abroad." *Journal of Planning History*, Feb. 2002: 6–28.

Mumford, Eric. "The 'Tower in a Park' in America: Theory and Practice." *Planning Perspectives* 10, no. 1 (1995): 17–41.

Mumford, Lewis. "A Modest Man's Enduring Contributions to Urban and Regional Planning." *AIA Journal* (Dec. 1976): 20–22.

———. "The Planned Community." *Architectural Forum* 58, no. 4 (Apr. 1933): 253–74.

National Park Service, "Roland Park Historic District," *Baltimore: A National Register of Historic Places Travel Itinerary*, Washington, D.C.: National Park Service, 2002.

Oberlander, H. Peter, and Eve Newbrun. *Houser: The Life and Work of Catherine Bauer*. Vancouver: University of British Columbia Press, 1999.

Parsons, Kermit C. "Clarence Stein and the Greenbelt Towns: Settling for Less." *American Planning Association Journal* 56, no. 2 (Spring 1990): 161–83.

———. "Collaborative Genius." *American Planning Association Journal* 60, no. 4 (Aug. 1994): 462–82.

———. ed. *The Writings of Clarence Stein: Architect of the Planned Community.* Baltimore: Johns Hopkins University Press, 1998.

Parsons, Kermit C., and David Schuyler, eds. *From Garden City to Green City: The Legacy of Ebenezer Howard.* Baltimore: Johns Hopkins University Press, 2002.

Peterson, Jon A. *The Birth of City Planning in the United States, 1840–1917.* Baltimore: Johns Hopkins University Press, 2003.

Plunz, Richard. *A History of Housing in New York City.* New York: Columbia University Press, 1990.

Pommer, Richard. "The Architecture of Urban Housing in the United States During the Early 1930s." *Journal of the Society of Architectural Historians* 37, no. 4 (Dec. 1978): 235–64.

Radford, Gail. *Modern Housing for America: Policy Struggles in the New Deal Era.* Chicago: University of Chicago Press, 1996.

Roth, Leland. *A Concise History of American Architecture.* New York: Harper and Row, 1979.

Saab, A. Joan. "Historical Amnesia: New Urbanism and the City of Tomorrow." *Journal of Planning History* 6, no. 3 (Aug. 2007): 191–213.

Sandweiss, Eric. *St. Louis: The Evolution of an American Urban Landscape.* Philadelphia: Temple University Press, 2001.

Schaffer, Daniel. *Garden Cities for America: The Radburn Experience.* Philadelphia: Temple University Press, 1982.

Schumann, Ulrich Maximilian. "The Hidden Roots of the Garden City Idea: From John Sinclair to John Claudius Loudon." *Journal of Planning History*, Nov. 2003, 291–310.

Seidenberg, Mel. "Chatham Village Co-op Will Convert to Ownership Plan." *Pittsburgh Post-Gazette*, Jan. 30, 1960.

Sneff, Alice Hogg. "Manager Keeps Tenants Contented." *Pittsburgh Sun-Telegraph*, June 5, 1935.

Starrett, C. V. "Old Bigham House Has Romantic History." *Chatham Village News*, Dec. 1932, reprinted in *Chatham Village News,* Fiftieth Anniversary Edition, Oct. 10, 1982, 1.

"State Housing: American Style." *Fortune* 9, no. 2 (Feb. 1934): 26–33.

Steig, Bill. "Housing Project, 30s Gem, Thrives Quietly Amid City." *Pittsburgh Post-Gazette*, Jul. 26, 1980, 15.

Stein, Clarence S. "Building Homes as Unit Project Gives Harmony." *New York Herald-Tribune*, Sept. 14, 1930.

———. "The Case for New Towns." *Planners Journal*, Mar.–June 1939, 39–44.

———. "City Patterns . . . Past." *New Pencil Points*, June 1942, 52–56.

———. "Community Planning and Architecture." *New York Times*, Jul. 23, 1933.

———. "Destructive Housing vs. Constructive Housing." *Architecture*, May 1933.

———. "Henry Wright: 1878–1936." *American Architect and Architecture*, Aug. 1936, 23–24.

———. "Housing and the Depression." *Octagon: A Journal of the American Institute of Architects* 5, no. 6 (June 1933), 4.

———. "Housing the People." *Nation*, Mar. 10, 1926.

———. "Investment Housing Pays." *Survey Graphic*, Feb. 1940, 75–77.

———. "New Towns for the Needs of a New Age." *New York Times Magazine*, Oct. 1933.

———. Papers and Letters. Division of Rare Books and Manuscripts Collections. Kroch Library, Cornell University, Ithaca, NY.

———. *Toward New Towns for America.* Cambridge, MA: MIT Press, 1951; rev. ed., 1957.

Stein, Clarence S., and Albert Mayer. "New Towns and Fresh In-City Communities." *Architectural Record*, Aug. 1964, 129–38.

Stephenson, Bruce. "The Roots of the New Urbanism: John Nolen's Garden City Ethic." *Journal of Planning History* (May 2002): 99–123.

Sussman, Carl, ed. *Planning the Fourth Migration: The Neglected Vision of the Regional Planning Association of America.* Cambridge, MA: MIT Press, 1976.

Szylvian, Kristin M. "Bauhaus on Trial: Aluminum City Terrace and Federal Defense Housing Policy During World War II." *Planning Perspectives* 9, no. 3 (1994): 229–54.

Szylvian Bailey, Kristin. "Defense Housing in Greater Pittsburgh: 1945–1955." *Pittsburgh History*, Spring 1990: 16–28.

Unwin, Raymond. *Town Planning in Practice: An Introduction to the Art of Designing Cities and*

Suburbs. New York: Charles Scribner's Sons, 1909.

Vater, David J. "Chatham Village: A Bibliography" Unpublished manuscript, 1994.

———. "Chatham Village Historic District." National Register of Historic Places Registration Form. Washington, D.C.: U.S. Department of the Interior, National Park Service, 1997.

"Village Here Being Sold in Co-op Deal." *Mt. Washington News*, Jan. 8, 1960, 1, 8.

von Hoffman, Alexander. "The End of the Dream: The Political Struggle of America's Public Housers." *Journal of Planning History* 4, no. 3 (Aug. 2005): 222–53.

Wallace, Edith B., and Paula S. Reed, with Linda McClelland. "Chatham Village National Historic Landmark Nomination." Washington, D.C.: U.S. Department of the Interior, National Park Service, 2003. http://www.nps .gov/nhl/designations/samples/pa/ Chatham%20Village.pdf.

Wright, Gwendolyn. *Building the Dream: A Social History of Housing in America*. Cambridge, MA: MIT Press, 1981.

Wright, Henry. "Are We Ready for an American Housing Advance?" *Architecture* 67 (June 1933): 309–16.

———. "The Autobiography of Another Idea." *Western Architect* 39, no. 9 (Sept. 1930): 137–53.

———. "Hillside Group Housing." *Architectural Record* 72, no. 4 (Oct. 1932): 221–30.

———. "Hillside Group Housing: Chatham Village." *Architecture* 68 (Aug. 1933).

———. Papers. Division of Rare Books and Manuscripts Collections. Kroch Library, Cornell University, Ithaca, NY.

———. *Rehousing Urban America*. New York: Columbia University Press, 1935.

Illustration Credits

All photos are taken by, and appear courtesy of, Angelique Bamberg, except as noted below:

American Architect and Architecture (February 1937): 4.3

Architectural Forum (March 1932): 1.2, 2.7, 2.10, 2.11, 3.11

Architectural Forum (January 1935): 1.3, 1.4

Architectural Forum (October 1941): 5.5

Architectural Record (October 1931): 2.17, 2.18, 6.2

Architecture (August 1916): 2.3

Architecture (September 1926): 2.4

Carnegie Library of Pittsburgh: 1.7

Chatham Village Archives: 2.14, 3.7, 3.10, 3.12, 3.13, 3.15, 3.22, 3.24, 3.25, 6.6

Greater Astoria Historical Society: 2.8

Firth, Robert, and Informing Design, Inc., © Informing Design, Inc.: front matter map

Howard, Ebenezer. *Garden Cities of To-morrow* (1898): 2.1

House and Home (May 1956): 1.5

Historic American Engineering Record, Library of Congress: 5.4

Library and Archives Division, Sen. John Heinz History Center: frontispiece, 3.1, 3.18, 2.15, 2.16, 3.4, 3.5, 3.6, 3.14, 3.20, 3.21, 3.23, 4.2, 4.8, 4.12, 4.6, 4.7, 4.9, 4.10, 4.11, 4.13, 4.14, 5.1, 5.6, 6.8, 6.9

Olmsted, Vaux, and Co. Landscape Architects (1869): 2.2

Pencil Points (January 1940): 1.6, 3.2, 3.17

Pittsburgh City Photographer Collection, 1901–2002), AIS.1971.05, Archives Service Center, University of Pittsburgh: 1.1, 4.1

Pittsburgh-Post Gazette, Copyright ©, 2010, all rights reserved. Reprinted with permission. 4.15

Stein, Clarence S. *Toward New Towns for America* (MIT Press, 1951): 2.5, 2.6, 2.9, 2.12, 2.13, 6.1

Toker, Franklin: 6.4

Index